Creating the Life You Want to Live:

From Average to Amazing in 30 Days

by Drema Dial, Ph.D.

Table of Contents

Introduction

Amazing things can happen in 30 days. Jack Kerouac sat down at his typewriter and banged out the first draft of On the Road. Zhang Yue, founder and chairman of China's Broad Sustainable Building Company, erected a 30-story building in half that time. A caterpillar can change into a butterfly — you can even expect to receive your tax refund from the IRS within 30 days after filing your return! You may be thinking, "But I don't want to write a novel. I just want to improve my life." And that's exactly what I was hoping your response would be. If a classic American novel can be written in 30 days, you can start changing your life for the better in the same amount of time. You are virtually guaranteed to see — sometimes amazing! — results.

Now I'm not trying to pass off this 30-day challenge idea as something new and novel. As I'm sure you're aware, there are plenty of 30-day challenges out there for you to choose from, whether you want to commit random acts of kindness for 30 days or detox your body. Why are they so popular? Because they allow you to "try on" a change, test the waters. And while thirty days is a sufficient amount of time to make an impact, it's not the rest of your life, which is important. Phrases like "the rest of your life" and "forever" tend to spook us, not to mention, they're hard concepts to wrap our brains around. But the hope is for you to be so pleased with your results after 30 days that your brain will say, "Yeah, I can make this a part of my life going forward."

Taking your life from average to amazing in 30 days may seem like an outrageous proposal. It most certainly is! And as I'll explain later, it's not as simple as that. But if you approach The Amazing 30 Day Challenge with the right attitude, you can expect to get different results than what you may have gotten with past attempts to make changes in your life. Why? Because The Amazing 30 Day Challenge is not one-size-fits all: you have input. You pick your main objective for the challenge and lay out your plan to achieve it; I give you the tools and information you need to do so. Plus, I offer some assignments chosen for their ability to motivate regardless of your particular goal or change. If you lose your focus along the way, just get back on track the next day. Don't let yourself off the hook. If you stick with it, your confidence will slowly start to build, your optimism will grow and your commitment's going to get stronger. Believe you can do this! There's only one catch: it's not going to be easy. And it may very well take longer than 30 days for you to get the results you ultimately want. There, I said it.

How's that sitting with you?

You're probably saying to yourself, "But the book title implies that I can create the life I want to live in 30 days. That is false advertising!" Fair enough. Just hear me out.

The cold, hard truth is change is hard. Saying you want to make changes and actually doing it are two different things. In 30 days, you can create the conditions for the life you want, but it may take longer for you to be inhabiting that life. And while change can be exciting and liberating, it's also uncomfortable and can be downright painful at times. There are no quick fixes when it comes to changing long-worn habits of thinking and behavior, no matter what popular culture might lead you to believe. There's no magic number when it comes to making sustainable changes or breaking what for some might be lifelong patterns. But the 21- to 30-day myth is very powerful — and appealing!

Depending on what you want to accomplish, it may take less than 30 days to imprint a change. Multiply that by two, and you'll have the number of days it could take for many of us to retrain our brains; for others it may take substantially longer. Which leads me back to those earlier examples. Yes, Kerouac did sit down and type out the first draft of his novel in 20 days. But it took Harper Lee over two years to pen To Kill a Mockingbird. And even though the pupal stage of the Monarch Butterfly is 9-14 days, for the Indra Swallowtail it's 11 months! It's going to be different for everyone, and at some point you're just going to want to BE THERE. You may even be tempted to give up. But I'm going to paraphrase your parents on a road trip, "You'll be there when you get there."

Here's what I can tell you: those first 30 days are usually the toughest but they are also probably the most rewarding. During that time you'll start to feel a shift, and that's why I strongly encourage you to commit to The Amazing 30 Day Challenge to kick off your transformation. If you do so, you will have laid the foundation for a life you will love to live. If that is what you truly want, just put your head down, do the work and withstand a little discomfort along the way. Perseverance is something we tend to undervalue in American culture in favor of instant gratification. But if you can become skilled at persevering and take to heart the idea that practice makes the master, you can change your thinking, your behavior and ultimately, your life. My bottom line: if you're looking for something quick and easy, my way isn't it. But if you're looking for tools and methods that have been proven effective over years of counseling hundreds of patients, then read on.

Before we talk about how you can create the life you've always wanted, let's look at how you've created the life you never wanted … or at the least, a life that could use improvement. To facilitate this, I've created The Dial Dialogues™, a simple four-step process designed to hone in on your aspirations and desires, and identify and eliminate the obstacles to your fulfilling them. You can use this tool whether you want to learn a new language or start an exercise program. If you're always busy but feel like you never get anything accomplished, this exercise will be very useful to you. To get started, grab a notebook and something to write with, and keep them handy as you continue reading. (If you're technologically inclined, there are some terrific apps to help you stay on track. Just use the search term, "healthy habits apps." For our purposes, I'll just reference using your pen and paper.)

The Dial Dialogues™

1. Determine How You Spend Your Time

How do you spend your time on a routine basis? Please answer the following questions as honestly as possible:

1. How many hours per week do you log mindlessly surfing the Internet?

2. How much time do you spend watching television?

3. How much time do you spend texting friends or dealing with personal e-mail?

4. How much time do you spend on Facebook or other social networking sites?

5. How much time do you spend on "non-essential" tasks?

6. How much time do you spend sleeping during daylight hours?

7. How often are you burdened by thoughts of what you could or should be doing?

8. How much time do you spend wishing your life were different?

I encourage you to track the amount of time you devote to these activities 7–10 days prior to beginning The Amazing 30 Day Challenge. The last two are a little harder to quantify, but the point is for you to start being able to see all of the activities that fill up your current life. Don't judge your responses, just acknowledge them for the time being. Writing down your answers and making notes on your feelings and actions is an important part of this process, and it will be directly related to how successful you are in creating the life you want. Studies show, for example, that dieters who keep a food diary lose more weight than those who don't. When you track how you use your time, you will instantly start to see your patterns, which will help you understand why and when you typically engage in certain behaviors. It's important to identify which behaviors are occasional and which are habitual. The difference? Habitual behaviors have sneaky ways of becoming obstacles to personal growth. They can make us ineffective, inefficient and unproductive. Which can lead to stagnation. Which can lead to a rut. And when you find yourself stuck in a rut, those stealthy little habits are right in there with you. There's an old Texas saying that goes, "If all you ever do is all you've ever done, then all you'll ever get is all you ever got." So, the $64,000 question is: What have you been up to lately?

2. Figure Out What It Is You Really Want

In order to begin creating a life you'll love living, you first need to ask yourself what it is you want out of life. You might think you know, but when you examine this question in more depth, your true desires may surprise you. Some things may seem obvious: most of us want to love and be loved, to feel supported, to feel safe and secure, to be "happy." But it's more complicated than it seems. The love and support you want may be very different from your divorced friend's idea of love and support. The things that give you a sense of security may not be the same things your unemployed brother-in-law needs to feel secure. That's why you really need to take a closer look at this question.

Let's start with this idea of happiness. How do you define happiness? It's time to pull out your pen and paper again. Finish the following sentences:

- *I know I am happy when ...*

- *I feel happy when ...*

- *I think I'm happy when ...*

- *I'm happiest when ...*

Your answers may be similar for all four prompts, which is perfectly fine. The purpose of the exercise is simply to get you thinking more concretely about what makes you happy. Connections with other people are a major source of happiness for many individuals. Participating in an activity you find meaningful may also be a source of happiness. But what made you happy in your twenties may not make you happy in your forties. And while other people can be sources of happiness, your happiness shouldn't be dependent on other people. Because true happiness is found when you are present in your own life.

Now for each of those prompts, substitute the concepts of love, support and security. At the end of The Amazing 30 Day Challenge, answer these questions again. Your evolution might surprise you.

3. Acknowledge What's Stopping You from Achieving Your Goals

Over the years, clients have given me every reason imaginable for not making the changes they long to make in their lives. If you've used any of the following as a reason to justify the status quo in your life, write them in your notebook:

• *I've tried this before and I always fail.*

- *I start out strong but then something (beyond my control) happens to derail me and I lose my momentum.*

- *I just don't have the time!*

- *I want to change, but I don't know how.*

- *I'm too (fill in the blank: old, tired, heavy, shy, uncoordinated, scared, mistrustful, etc.).*

- *It feels (fill in the blank: selfish, conceited, like I'm taking time away from my family) if I'm focused on just me.*

It's easy to use the needs of others as reasons for not taking care of ourselves. I'm not going to tell you those personal, business or community responsibilities are not important, because they are. But what I'm encouraging you to do is to balance those commitments against your own spiritual, physical and emotional health. It goes back to being present in your own life. And making the simple decision to be as attentive to yourself as you are to the people and demands outside of you.

Perhaps you've "settled" for the life you're living because you're paralyzed by feelings of fear and loneliness or the despair that nothing will ever change, no matter what you do. Maybe somewhere along the way you lost your confidence or decided you couldn't trust yourself to make good decisions. That's the past, and you can't change that.

If you want to script a different future, you have to believe that you deserve a rich and fulfilling life as much as anyone else does. You may not be in that place yet, but know that the power to create it lies with you. I don't have that power, nor does any other therapist, psychologist or self-help guru. We can guide you, we can encourage you and some of us can even convince you that we have the "answers." Gather all the advice, tips and strategies that you want to: buy books, participate in therapy and take classes. Mull over different approaches, set the intent to make the change or changes, even set a date, but if you don't ever actually put the information you've learned to use, nothing is ever going to change.

4. Create a Plan for Success

Below I've laid out an action plan for implementing changes in your life. There is a wealth of research on goal setting theory and behavior modification, and if you've attempted to make changes before, you're familiar with these steps. My plan is a variation on widely accepted strategies.

1. Identify your specific intention or the behavior you want to change.

2. Write down your reasons for setting the intention or wanting to make the change in as much detail as possible.

3. Make a 30-day commitment.

4. Establish manageable goals.

5. Schedule non-negotiable time to be devoted to this change/goal and put it in your Smartphone or write it on your calendar.

6. Set up an incremental reward system.

7. Chart your progress.

So let's say you want to start doing yoga. Here's how that might look:

1. I am going to start practicing yoga on a regular basis.

2. I want to do yoga in order to become more strong and flexible. I want to feel good about following through with something I keep saying I will do. Practicing yoga will give me confidence, and I know I feel better when I'm attending yoga on a regular basis. I want to feel good naked!

3. I will commit to a regular yoga practice from September 1-30.

4. I will attend a class at my gym 4 times per week.

5. I will attend the 6 p.m. class on Mondays, Wednesdays and Fridays, and the Saturday morning class at 10 a.m. I will block these times out on my calendar just as I would any other appointment. I

will not rearrange my schedule to accommodate requests from other people.

6. At the end of every week in which I attend all of my scheduled classes, I will reward myself with a healthy smoothie at the café next to the gym, go see a movie with a friend or give myself an extra hour doing something I enjoy. These little rewards along the way will help keep me motivated.

7. I will create a handwritten or computer-generated chart of my yoga class schedule for the 30 days I've chosen and check off each class I attend. I'll record how I felt before the class, such as anticipation or resistance, and how I feel after following through and doing something good for my body and spirit.

There are some key guidelines for ensuring success. Your intention must be specific; simply saying you want to become more flexible or get in better shape is too vague and too broad. Also, make sure that the goals you set are achievable. In the above example, let's assume that you have practiced yoga in the past but maybe you have only been getting to class once or twice a week. If you have always wanted to attend yoga classes, maybe starting off going to four a week is a little ambitious.

You may have many changes you'd like to make in your life, but taking them all on at once can be overwhelming. And when you feel overwhelmed, it's often easiest to just do nothing. So choose just one major change to focus on during your Amazing 30 Day Challenge. If you do, you may notice something interesting start to happen: you'll also start making positive changes in other parts of your life without really thinking about it. So view this as an experiment. No pressure. Just commit to the program for 30 days. It will either be the jump-start you needed to launch you into your new life, or confirmation that you can't do it all by yourself. Maybe you'll decide you could use the help of a therapist, personal coach, fitness trainer or some other expert to support you. Or it's possible you'll decide to join a support group of individuals struggling with the same challenges you are. The only thing you can't do during or after the 30-day challenge is give up on yourself. That is not allowed. Because believe me, you are stronger than you think you are.

Committed? Go to www.theamazing30.com to sign up for 30 days of e-mail encouragement, tips, and motivation!

About *Creating the Life You Want to Live*

(and How to Get the Most out of the Book)

This book and its companion 30-day challenge came about as a natural extension of my counseling services, once I realized that many of my clients shared one common trait: a negative mindset. Each chapter in the book challenges a particular symptom of a negative mindset or examines a potential source of stress that can make you feel trapped in an unfulfilling life. Then I offer strategies for managing or eliminating those things that are standing between you and an amazing life.

The ten chapters have been arranged to build upon one another, and each is relatively short and easily digestible. My recommendation is to read through the entire book before beginning the program. Having said that, each chapter can also stand alone, so if you want to skip around, that's fine too. If there's a particular subject that catches your attention, start there and then continue wherever that leads you. There is a page for notes you may want to make after each chapter as well.

I've included "Real Life" scenarios in all of the chapters, so you can see how real people* I have counseled over the years have been able to break out of old habits and self-destructive behavior to start creating their amazing lives. Each chapter ends with a list of three Amazing Life Habits and one affirmation related to the chapter's topic. In the back of the book, you'll find easy to reference lists of Daily Affirmations and Amazing Life Habits.

The Amazing 30 Day Challenge is laid out at the end of the book, and it's pretty simple. Just remember, we're partners in this! As I mentioned earlier, you choose your challenge. Then I'll be prescribing supplements in the form of weekly assignments to keep you inspired, give you perspective and encouragement, and coax you out of your comfort zone. Every week, you'll have seven assignments: something to read, watch, write and do, all of which serve to support you and give you that little added motivation at critical points during the Challenge. (The "Watch" assignments are all courtesy of TED, which can be accessed at www.ted.com. If you are unfamiliar with the phenomenon that is TED, whose tagline is "Ideas Worth Spreading," then you are in for a treat! And even if you are, chances are I'll be introducing you to some speakers you haven't seen before.) It may seem a little daunting right now but it's doable. And yes, it's going to be difficult, but it's also going to be fun.

Your Amazing Life awaits! Let's get to it.

* Names of individuals featured in the "Real Life" scenarios have been changed to protect their privacy.

Chapter 1: What About Me?

The Importance of Self-Care

Everyone needs it. Most of us covet it. But so many men and women don't make time for self-care. This is time you set aside on a regular basis that's yours and yours alone. I understand how difficult it is to carve out that time. You may be a parent or be responsible for the support of aging parents. You may work part- or full-time. Then you have commitments outside of work: time with friends, volunteer work, and the things required to maintain normal life (grocery shopping, cleaning, etc.). It's easy to get overwhelmed, as we're being pushed and pulled in so many different directions. Some Mondays you may look at your schedule for the week and all you want to do is go back to bed. It's really about balance, a term which has become trite over the years, but you know what? It's a heck of a lot better than falling down day after day. And if you don't figure out what you need to recharge, relax, or reflect — whatever it is you need to do for yourself — then you will likely continue to fall down. Of course, you'll get back up and keep going, but how exhausting is that? It makes me tired just thinking about it.

Self-care looks different for everyone. Your "me" time may be simply sitting for five minutes and enjoying a cup of tea or coffee first thing in the morning, watching the world wake up through the window. It's surprising how centering five minutes of quiet contemplation can be. Maybe you have fifteen minutes in the morning? If you enjoy lingering over coffee, perfect. Or maybe you could squeeze in a short yoga or stretching session during that time, or watch a portion of a sports program or game you've recorded. This may be all you need on a daily basis, but I'd also suggest working in at least one monthly or weekly (even better!) date with yourself. Consider scheduling a monthly massage, signing up for a class, going to a museum or hitting golf balls — it's whatever you want to do.

Be prepared for the people in your life to push back. This happens sometimes. Once you start making time for yourself, someone in your life will react negatively: "You're going to be gone Thursday until 8? What about dinner?" Try to view their reactions as an opportunity to set boundaries and teach them about what you need. Because if they truly care about you, they will see you're rejuvenated by the time you're taking for yourself, and they will want you to have that time too. Maybe they will be encouraged to block out some of their own "me" time.

Real Life: John

John was feeling the effects of job burnout. By the time he came to see me, he wasn't enjoying anything anymore because as he put it, it felt like his life was being planned by someone else. And when John described his daily schedule to me, I was struck by how many appointments were on his calendar:

"Well, that's my boss; he and I meet twice a week to strategize. Those are events my wife plans for us, and these are all of my kids' events. That's a meeting with another consultant, this is a commitment I made to my brother." Just explaining it to me seemed to tire him.

"And you? Where are you in all of this?" I asked.

John looked at me uncomprehendingly. "I'm there, at all of those things! That's what I'm telling you."

John had fallen into the trap of showing up for everyone but himself. When I questioned him further, he admitted he had given up golf because it took up too much time, hadn't had a massage in ages, and that his workouts were sporadic. In short, John was no longer present in his own life, and his feelings of being burnt out and uninterested in anything were signs he was likewise not all there when he showed up for other people.

I asked him what was the one thing he felt he would really like to do. "Golf," he responded immediately, "but it takes up too much time." We began to brainstorm different ways he might be able to work golf back into his schedule — without causing him stress. John remembered there was a new golfing range in town with hourly rates. He decided to make this his first step and conferred with his wife about a time convenient for both of them.

"At first, she was concerned that it would mean more work for her, so we decided we would both have an evening for ourselves. I usually just go hit balls, but sometimes I'll call up someone I haven't seen for a while and have a beer. My wife was annoyed that I took my time every week while she didn't always take her evening. But last week, she admitted I seemed more relaxed and present when I'm home. Now, she's making it a point to do something she wants to do."

Although John's wife tried to be supportive, she initially had difficulty adjusting to his need to take time for himself. However, she soon saw how it benefited John. To John's credit, he maintained a boundary around the time he carved out for himself and truly enjoyed it. Although it might have been easier to give in when his wife wasn't happy with him, John stayed true to himself and did not return to old patterns of putting others before himself.

When we're feeling stressed or overwhelmed, we tend to fall back into patterns and behaviors that aren't necessarily good for us. Staying up too late, not sleeping well, pounding coffee and Red Bull all day just to keep up, and then crashing. Or maybe the cycle perpetuates itself and you take a sleeping pill so you can get that badly needed sleep. When you're just doing your best to keep up, that's when self-care usually falls by the wayside. Sleep is one of the best forms of self-care you can give yourself — and it costs nothing! It allows your body and your mind to reboot. When you don't get enough sleep, the stress hormone, cortisol, remains elevated and can set you up for a host of health problems. It's a vicious cycle. Yet, in today's fast-paced, online-based, 24-hour-news-cycle, instant-messaging world it's really hard to disengage from all technology to do something as boring as get to bed at a decent hour.

One thing you can do is to literally turn off any electronic devices 30-60 minutes before you turn out the light. Don't log in to Facebook right before you climb into bed, check messages on your smartphone or watch television right up until bedtime (and if you have a television in your bedroom, I beg you, consider moving it to a different room). Subjecting your brain to unnatural light and visual stimulation that amps up stress hormones and decreases calming hormones such as melatonin and serotonin right before you go to sleep? You remember the original "This is your brain on drugs" campaign from the eighties that featured the egg in the frying pan? It's a pretty powerful image — and you can just hear that egg sizzling, can't you? While I'm not trying to compare two hours spent watching the "The Bachelor" or checking your e-mail, Facebook and texting on your cell phone to doing heroin or cocaine (though some might say it can be just as bad for you in many ways), being plugged in all the time can change the way your brain works, affecting your mood, memory and behavior. Give your brain a break from the digital deluge at night, whether it's the TV, your computer or phone, and it will pay off, I promise. You also need to look at what's causing the stress and address that. Better ways of dealing with stress will help eliminate some of those self-destructive thoughts and behaviors that may be keeping you up at night.

Amazing Life Habits

- *Carve out time each week to do something you truly enjoy.*

- *Get 7-9 hours of sleep each night.*

- *Turn off electronic devices 30-60 minutes before turning in for the night.*

Daily Affirmation

I have the right to take time for myself to do things I enjoy.

NOTES:

Chapter 2: Detox Your Environment

The Stress of Mess

One thing that is inextricably linked to your well-being and also related to self-care is the condition of your environment. Your environment can be both a manifestation and a source of internal chaos and stress. At the same time, a welcoming and peaceful environment can have a calming and therapeutic effect on inner turmoil. Your environment is an extension of you, and if you're feeling stressed, overwhelmed or generally out of synch with life, your environment probably reflects that.

For example, have you stopped making efforts to make your home a welcome, inviting place to be? A place where you feel like you can have sanctuary, quiet, calmness, whatever you need? This is something that seems to happen almost overnight. You feel like you have things under control at home but then realize there are still loads of laundry waiting to be folded and put away, and a stack of mail, bills and other papers on the desk that need to be dealt with. The mess becomes the proverbial albatross 'round your neck.

Now, I will acknowledge that one person's chaos is another person's "organizational system." If a messy desk tells you you've been productive, then keep it. If I call you and ask, "Can I have that thingamajig back that I loaned you two weeks ago?" and you know that it's located third from the bottom in the pile of unrelated thingamajigs in your kitchen, then I would be hard-pressed to find fault with your system. On the other hand, that would drive some people up a wall. If you're one of those people, you probably clean and organize everything within an inch of its life when you're stressed because it helps you feel in control. In either case, it's working for you. But if being confronted with clutter and disarray triggers anxiety or stress in your mind, then you need to make it your priority to address it.

When something is noted as stress by our mind, we do everything in our power to avoid it. Rather than sitting down and paying bills, we toss the bills onto the desk (or find a new place) and then we avoid going through them as the pile gets bigger and bigger. Soon, we might begin avoiding the room itself, but even with the door closed, the desk still stalks us. Then, the voice in our head starts up with the nagging and shaming. Taken to an extreme, this can lead to missed payments, late fees and other embarrassing incidents. All to avoid the messy desk.

Real Life: Matty

Matty came to therapy to deal with what she called her "messy mind." She recounted how she frequently lost things — like her phone — and forgot dates she'd made with friends. She wondered if she had Attention Deficit Hyperactivity Disorder or was headed into dementia at the age of 34. I discovered she grew up in a home with emotionally distant parents who rarely paid attention to her. Most of her dad's attention went to the TV while her mom, exhibiting classic hoarding behavior, tended to large collections of things. Stacks of books, magazines, and photo albums lined the walls; boxes of toys, clothing, electronics and shoes were everywhere. The only space not invaded by her mother's collections was Matty's room.

Matty admitted her current home was "pretty messy." Her feelings about the disorder were similar to those she experienced as a child. "I was always stressed out and afraid that one of my friends might come by. That's the same way I feel now, only this time it's me who's the source of the stress!" While we continued to explore the deeper roots of her stress, we tackled the mess itself.

The plan we came up with required only two things of Matty at first: 1) She would commit to 15 minutes of de-cluttering every day, and 2) before her time started she would write down all of the reasons why she didn't want to do it.

As I had anticipated, Matty showed a lot of resistance in the first two weeks. She "forgot" to record her objections or "didn't have time" to spend 15 minutes de-cluttering. Fortunately, she and I had talked about the possibility of this happening ahead of time. I asked her to simply notice when resistance reared its head and to be curious about it so we could discuss it her sessions.

The exercise proved enlightening. "I'm afraid of change," Matty confessed. "I know what it's like to be stressed out. And, I also discovered that having a messy house keeps me safe because when I can't ask people over, I don't have to deal with the rejection that might come."

Then in the third week, something shifted.

"I followed the plan and it worked! I wrote down each day why I didn't want to work on my house, and then I just did it. It felt good! I really feel proud of my progress. Three times I actually worked for over an hour because I just got caught up in what I was doing," Matty excitedly told me. It was empowering for her to take control of the mess and her home. She experienced a decrease in her stress level and as we continued to work together, she also experienced a greater sense of well-being. She began to open up to the possibility of inviting people to her house because it was no longer a stress zone.

Amazing Life Habits

- *Institute a daily 15-minute de-cluttering practice.*

- *When you get the mail, deal with it immediately. That may mean sitting down right then and there to pay bills, toss or file, or putting the mail in a designated area to be taken care of later on a day of the week you've designated.*

• *Clean out the inside of your car weekly, and consider treating her to a good wash every other month. Your car is meant to get you from one place to another safely and shouldn't serve as a trash can, closet or storage space.*

Daily Affirmation

Physical clutter blocks the path to the life I want to live.

NOTES:

Chapter 3: Inhale, Exhale

Regaining Control One Breath at a Time

One thing that gets in the way when it comes to dealing with daily life is stress. It may be the stress of mess for one person or the anxiety around family dynamics for another, but we all have it. And in those moments when you're feeling particularly unraveled, overwhelmed or just plain frustrated, it can be really hard to do anything but let yourself be swallowed up by the emotion, which often renders you completely ineffective. The pressure may express itself as tears (more often in women as opposed to men) or anger, or may cause you to withdraw into yourself. Interactions with other human beings can be particularly aggravating. If you've ever suffered from I-Should-Have-Said-That Syndrome, then you know what I'm talking about. The stressful feelings and emotions are often worsened by the ruminating that occurs afterward, which frequently leads to the anger and frustration being directed inward for not having dealt with the situation on the spot and standing up for yourself.

Of course, you're able to come up with the snappy comeback or the dramatic exit much later, after the amygdala, your "survival" brain, has calmed down and your prefrontal cortex, responsible for rational thought, is in control again. But in that instant, when your anxiety level goes up, your body is flooded with adrenaline, and oxygen and blood flow are directed to the parts of your brain and body you'll need to use to deal with the threat at hand. The contemplative prefrontal cortex is not much help in these situations, unfortunately. Your heart beats faster, your breathing gets shallow, your muscles tense up, and you may perspire. It's an ingenious yet primitive response designed to protect us from mortal danger. However, most situations in which you are experiencing this physiological response, your life is not in jeopardy. Your sympathetic nervous system, which controls your body's fight-or-flight response, doesn't know this though. The alarm bells are going off, so it goes into overdrive. In so doing, it overwhelms the parasympathetic nervous system, which oversees such mundane tasks as breathing, digestion and elimination. These two tonically active systems counterbalance each other, so when the sympathetic nervous system puts us into a hyper state of arousal too often, it can lead to a host of chronic conditions and illnesses, which I won't list here because it will just stress you out. Needless to say, none of these conditions are included in the manual for an amazing life. But there are techniques you can use to get your brain out of survival mode more quickly, regain your faculties and protect your health.

Real Life: Kate

Kate's relationship with her boss was, as she described it, "difficult." A common scenario involved him summoning her to his office after not having spoken to her for weeks. He would then say to her, "I don't understand why you did this, and I want an explanation." In every instance, she was always completely caught of guard by these conversations because up until each confrontation, she had felt confident and satisfied with her work performance. So, Kate would understandably get defensive and say something she would regret, which resulted in further tension between her and her boss.

From where I sat, it looked like her future at this particularly company was in serious jeopardy if she didn't address the communication problems with her supervisor. I started by asking her to pay attention to her physiological response: what was her body experiencing at the moment she was face to face with her boss? She realized her palms began to sweat and she could feel herself getting hot. In her case, it was physically obvious because her lower jaw, neck and chest would turn bright red. Humiliated and embarrassed, she felt compelled to defend herself and would end up saying something she didn't really mean, which made things worse.

I suggested Kate use her physical responses as her cue to remove herself from the situation to regain her composure. At the moment she started to feel the heat rising and her palms begin to perspire, she would say to her boss, "Excuse me, I need to take just a moment." Then she would step outside the office and do some breathing exercises to calm herself down. Your heart rate is not something you can directly control, but your breathing? Now there's something you can control. And by breathing slowly and deeply, you strengthen the parasympathetic nervous system so that it can reign in the sympathetic nervous system and restore the natural balance.

Though awkward at first, this technique worked well for Kate, and her boss commended her on taking the steps to improve their interactions, which not surprisingly, made a huge difference in their relationship. Taking those few moments allowed Kate to return to the discussion with a cool head and leave her defensiveness at the door. It also really boosted her self-confidence because she realized she had the power to change the situation. She couldn't always control that initial reaction at being called to the boss's office, but when she felt herself starting to feel anxious, she knew that she had the tools to get herself back under control.

Breathing is something we take for granted. We don't have to think about it because the autonomic nervous system (comprising the sympathetic, parasympathetic and enteric systems) takes care of it for is. Breathing exercises force you to be more mindful by bringing your awareness to your breath. The exercises are relatively easy to learn, and you can do them anywhere, at any time. Breathing exercises have been shown to be extremely effective in managing the affects of both acute and chronic stress.

Breath is empowering — after all, it is the life force! And when you realize the health benefits of these exercises, just as with any other form of exercise, you will want to make them a regular part of your daily routine.

Below is a simple diaphragmatic breathing exercise you can do sitting or standing in a relaxed position, or lying down. Note that inhalation requires more energy, so the exhalation, the release, is when we start to induce relaxation.

1. Place one hand on your chest and one hand on your abdomen. As you breathe, be aware of making the hand on your abdomen push out beyond the hand on your chest.

2. Slowly inhale through your nose for a count of four, breathing into your abdomen and causing it to expand.

3. Slowly exhale through your mouth for a count of four, pushing the breath out of your lungs by contracting your stomach.

4. Pause briefly after each exhalation.

5. Repeat two-three times.

If you can extend your exhalation to the count of eight, it's even more beneficial, but this may require some practice. That's basically it — easy, right? Breathing exercises are also great to do right before you go to bed if you suffer from insomnia or have difficulty falling asleep. If you watch infants or toddlers sleep, they do this diaphragmatic breathing automatically. It's only later that chest breathing becomes the norm. So to help relax your body and mind before sleep, lie down, placing one hand on your chest and one hand on your abdomen. Breathe deeply into your belly; the hand on your abdomen should rise higher than the hand on your chest. When you're in a supine position with your hands resting in this way, it will be clear to you whether or not you're doing the exercise correctly. Focusing on your breath in this position will be helpful to you when you employ the technique at other times. If you happen to fall asleep while you're doing the exercise, then you're doing it right! And you'll likely wake feeling more rested. I highly recommend doing a few cycles before bed to release the tension of the day or, if you have more time, practice for several minutes as a form of meditation. And if you have the opportunity to attend a yoga class or to do some other form of mind-body exercise, such as Qi Gong or Tai Chi, during the day, seize it!

Amazing Life Habits

- *Take 10-15 minutes at the beginning or end of each day for a breathing meditation.*

- *Take care of your lungs. If you smoke, make it your priority to be an ex-smoker.*

- *When confronted with a person or situation that stresses you out, take a moment to calm down with a few cycles of breathing exercises before speaking or acting.*

Daily Affirmation

With every full breath I collect positive energy and expel all discomfort and negativity.

NOTES:

Chapter 4: Lather, Rinse, Repeat

The Power of Habit

A habit is a pattern of behavior, established through repetition, that we often do without thinking. Habits can be saboteurs or champions, and they can be oh-so-hard to change. Why? Because to change them we have to be mindful. We aren't always aware when we're making a habit, and once the autopilot in our brain has been engaged and the habit is set, our brain is freed up to focus on other things. No conscious thought needed to brush your teeth, turn off the lights in a room upon leaving, or drive a familiar route. But there are a couple of things you should know when attempting to change a habit. It's usually harder to break a bad/unhealthy habit than it is to make a new/positive habit. This is mainly because a lot of things that are not good for us are addictive in nature, affecting the pleasure centers of our brain that release the feel-good hormone, dopamine.

When trying to break an unhealthy habit, many people are successful if they replace that habit with a healthy habit acting upon the same area of the brain (that's why exercise is often a healthy substitute habit). You won't be successful if you go into it half-heartedly; you need to commit 110%. As I discussed earlier, it may take longer for the new behavior to become a bona fide habit or for the old behavior to release its hold on you, but if you stick with it, you will be rewarded.

So now I'm going to put you in the hot seat: Do you have a particular habit or behavior that you've resolved to change time and again only to find yourself falling back into the same familiar pattern? Though there are some people who can set their mind to do or not do something and seemingly follow through with little effort, that's not most of us. Relying solely on willpower sets you up for failure and then you feel bad about yourself because you weren't "strong" enough. That's why it's essential for you to have a strategy in place to help you break old habits and establish new ones. Imagine this common scenario: You had planned to come home and exercise after work. But what did you end up doing? Grabbing a snack (just for some quick energy), changing clothes (but somehow, they're not your workout clothes) and then it's 1½ hours later, and you're sitting in front of the television with an empty bag of Cheetos. How did that happen?

This is the part where we do a dramatic reenactment of your actions from the time you get home from work to the time you realize the workout is not going to happen. In The Power of Habit, Charles Duhigg shares the discoveries of researchers at MIT about habit formation. The process features three distinct parts: a cue, a routine and a reward. Once you identify the particulars of your own habit loop, you can begin substituting new positive behaviors for the old ones.

The easiest first step is to identify your routine. What did you do when you first walked in the house? The second your key turned the lock and you walked in the door, your brain probably kicked into autopilot. The conversation in your head may have gone something like this: "Boy, I'm starving — I deserve a little pick-me-up after my long stressful day at work. Ooh, that gigantic blueberry muffin will do the trick. It will give me a little carb boost for the workout — not the best choice but it's okay this one time, right? Now let's get changed for this workout — boy this muffin hits the spot! Hmmm … it's probably a little too warm to work out in sweatpants, but there they are, right there on the chair where I left them yesterday. They'll do — I'll burn more calories because I'll sweat more, plus, I forgot to put my exercise clothes in the dryer last night. Okay where are my shoes? I think they're under the couch in the living room. While I'm lacing up my shoes, I'll just catch up on the news — why not, I'm not in a hurry. Wow, that actor got arrested again? Wonder what the story is there?"

Now you've gotten conveniently distracted from your original objective and your brain remains on autopilot for the rest of the evening. This is your habit loop. You may have had the best of intentions but when you walked in the door, your brain railroaded you into your old pattern of behavior, "This is what we do. We get a snack, we change into comfy clothes, and we slump onto the couch in front of the television for the rest of the evening." There's no real conscious decision making going on here. You've practiced this routine for so long, your brain isn't willing to give it up so easily. And there's a reason why.

When your brain goes on autopilot, allowing you to follow a routine without thinking about it, what it's really doing is conserving energy. It's conserving energy for something requiring more conscious thought, something more important. In that sense, habits have actually been a highly useful tool in our evolutionary development. When we attempt to learn something new, if we consistently practice and reinforce the information or behavior, it eventually becomes second nature to us. Which is great if you're trying to become fluent in a language or become a world-class pitcher, but not so great when you're trying to do something like quit smoking or give up unhealthy foods. In order to identify and anticipate the cues for the undesirable behavior and create new ones to inspire the desired behavior, you have to pay attention and turn off your brain's autopilot.

In the previous example, it's important to acknowledge that just walking into your house after work may set the old pattern into motion for you at this time. So one strategy might be for you to take your exercise clothes to your workplace and change before you leave. That doesn't mean you have to go to the gym, but it gives you the option to bypass your house. Maybe you still drive home, but now that you're dressed to exercise, you might tell yourself, "I'm going for a walk around the neighborhood right now because I know that if I enter my house, I'm less likely to follow through on the walk." If hunger is a cue that sets you off course, replacing the unhealthy snacks with a healthier choice that you can throw in your bag or briefcase when you leave the house in the morning, will help you avoid temptation. After completing your walk, give yourself a pat on the back. You may think, "But it's only a short walk. Big deal." It is a big deal because you've completed the first step toward your goal of exercising rather than being a couch potato after work.

In establishing new habits, positive reinforcement is important for internal motivation. Some people might brush off such a seemingly small accomplishment. But think about how children learn: The child attempts a few steps and is met with delight and praise. He internalizes this good feeling and takes more steps. Or tries to ride a bike. Despite falling and wobbling, if his efforts are met with praise rather than derision, he is likely to continue learning until he masters bike riding. It's similar for adults learning in new areas or attempting to create a new habit. We still need acknowledgement and praise, but we can do this for ourselves. And in so doing, we can begin to re-route our neural pathways away from the conditioned thoughts of why we can't, won't or shouldn't. Telling ourselves, "Great job!" lights up the reward center in the brain, creating that good feeling we want more of, which in turn, positively affects our behavior.

When breaking or establishing a new habit, it's important to be mindful and be prepared. Research shows that if you set up a plan — referred to as an "implementation intention" in psychology — you can start making the conscious decisions needed to break the habit loop. For example, you set out your workout clothes the night before, you throw away the less healthy foods in the house, you sign up and pay for an exercise class online — whatever it is that you need to do to make it easier on yourself to make the change you desire.

Real Life: Peter

"Every day I eat a healthy lunch. Then somewhere in the middle of the afternoon, I get this craving for something sweet. Every day I tell myself, 'I've had my lunch; I'm not going to do that.' But sure enough, somewhere between three and four o'clock, I get up, I go to the vending machine and I get something that's really not healthy for me."

He identified the habit, including the part where he tells himself, "I'm not going to do this." Now what he needed to do in order to change was to identify the cue. At this time of day, many people experience an afternoon slump, especially those who work in an office at a computer all day. Usually it happens between 2 and 4 p.m., when your brain and body energy tends to dip. It may be caused by eating habits, natural circadian rhythms or even boredom. Was this need for a sugar boost a subconscious effort to wake his brain up? Was he not eating enough for lunch so he was truly feeling hungry? Perhaps he simply glanced at the clock around this time, which triggered the automatic pilot in his brain: "Time to go to the vending machine." Before he knows it, he's back at his desk, back to work, munching on a bag of M&Ms and thinking his craving was being satisfied. But had it?

I asked Peter exactly what his routine was: Did he take the same route to the vending machine? Did he purchase the same snack every day? After some thought, Peter realized what he really looked forward to was the break from his computer and the chance to stretch his legs. And he usually stopped along the way to chat briefly with colleagues, as well. We began to suspect that his reward, rather than the sugary or salty snack, was the mental break and chance to socialize. So I asked Peter to start taking an apple as his afternoon snack and to use it as his cue to stand and stretch, and to take a few minutes to engage in conversation with co-workers.

Two weeks later, Peter reported he'd only gone to the vending machine once, on a day he'd forgotten to bring a piece of fruit. Because he recognized that a food craving wasn't the primary motivation for his afternoon trips to the vending machine, he was able to substitute a healthy snack for an unhealthy snack, a new habit he was able to adopt with relative ease!

Amazing Life Habits

- *Before trying to replace an old habit or establish a new one, identify possible obstacles to your success and create a plan to overcome them.*

- *Drive a different route to or from work a few days per week. This will help turn off your brain's autopilot—especially important when you're in control of 3,500 or more pounds of metal!*

- *Replace one unhealthy behavior with something healthy. Follow Peter's example, and make M&Ms the backup plan or a once-in-awhile treat rather than the norm.*

Daily Affirmation

I feel strong and good about myself when I follow through on my intentions.

NOTES:

Chapter 5: Your Brilliant Disguise

Tips from the Self-Confidence Toolbox

"Sticks and stones may break my bones but words will never hurt me." How many times did you respond to childhood taunts with this familiar rhyme? In the moment, it felt good to have a ready-made retort. It might have briefly made you feel superior because you were taking the high road and rising above the name calling and bullying. But as we all know, words do matter and sometimes they can hurt. And if we're particularly vulnerable when a piece of criticism is lobbed at us, it can stay with us far longer than it should and have lifelong effects. The voice of that person, whether a loved one, an enemy or even a stranger, may lie mute until a time when we're feeling insecure and a situation arises that awakens the part of our brain that likes to remind us we're not good enough. And the lower we're striking on the self-confidence scale, the easier it is to believe the negative stuff about ourselves.

If I were to ask you today to name two things you like about yourself, what would you say? I hope that given a few minutes, you would be able to come up with at least two things. By the end of The Amazing 30 Day Challenge, I trust you'll be able to list at least ten, if not more. Now if nothing comes to mind right away, then this is obviously a question that deserves further exploration. Start with something obvious, like a physical characteristic — maybe you like your smile or your toned arms. Go a little deeper and perhaps there's a character trait, a talent or a skill you possess that you could pat yourself on the back for. It's important to remind ourselves about our positive qualities because most of us are quick on the draw with the negative self-talk. We're usually much harder on ourselves than we are on others. You wouldn't say to your friend, "Oh my God! You look old and tired today!" But I bet you've had a day when you've looked into the mirror and said it to yourself. We all have those days. And that's okay. That's life. Just don't get in a boxing match with yourself every day. You can be your own best friend or your worst enemy. It's not about what other people say about you, it's what you tell yourself that can make or break you.

In both men and women, self-confidence is sexy and alluring. When I see a person who is obviously comfortable with himself and his place in the world, I'm intrigued. I wonder, "What's his secret?" A confident person exudes an energy that draws you in. I'm not talking about the life-of-the-party extrovert whom everyone loves and who captivates men and women wherever he goes. Neither am I talking about someone who is braggadocios or boastful, for that's not true confidence. The most self-assured people I know have a quiet confidence about them. You can identify them by the way they carry themselves and how they interact with other people. They care most about the opinions of the people in their lives who truly matter to them, not the masses. You would be hard-pressed to get them to speak negatively about someone else, and they will not sit idly by while someone else does. They generally hold an optimistic outlook on life and are resilient in the face of adversity.

Self-confidence is essential to living an amazing life, and in fact, to creating an amazing life. All of the lifestyle changes I recommend in the book will have an impact on your self-confidence with time and consistency. If you want to be the person whom other people see and think, "She really has it together. I want to get to know her," then you will be headed in the right direction if you commit to this program for 30 days. But you may be asking, "What about right now? Is there anything I can do to help my self-confidence today and change how people see me?" The answer is a resounding, "Yes!" Keep reading and you'll learn some simple things you can do that will cause others to take notice and also make you feel more self-assured. First you pretend, then eventually you become a master. But it takes practice, practice, practice.

One habit that helps many people in boosting their self-confidence is to create a daily intention. It might reflect a state of being you want to reinforce, your potential or a personal goal. A simple one to start with might be, "I am confident and attractive." Now, some people are very motivated by affirmations and some are completely turned off by them and regard them as a silly waste of time. If you hear the word "affirmation" and you immediately think of touchy-feely, woo-woo New Age nonsense, I get it. If you tell yourself, "I am confident and attractive," for 30 days, does that mean you're going to truly feel confident and attractive on day 31? Of course not.

Positive affirmations will only get you so far, but affirmations supported by positive action have real potential to improve your self-confidence, and promote optimism and hope for the future. So, maybe a more action-oriented affirmation would work for you, such as "I am working toward achieving my goals," or "I am changing my life in positive ways." And here's a tip to make this medicine go down easier, if you are having a hard time envisioning yourself practicing daily affirmations: have some self-compassion. Let's say your affirmation is our first example. If you say to yourself, "I am confident and attractive," but what you're really thinking is, "I can't complete a sentence and I look like a hot mess," that's okay. Own your feeling, repeat your affirmation and move on. If it helps, remind yourself that you were up late providing a shoulder for a friend to cry on. Maybe you've been working nights all week to make a deadline at work, and your brain is fried. Or hell, you did just celebrate your 35th birthday. But do you really want to go back to your twenties, even if your memory was sharp as a tack and you could bounce out of bed after staying up all night looking fresh as a daisy? Daily affirmations can be a nice complement to your Amazing 30 Day Challenge assignments and can spark the process of realigning your expectations and beliefs for the long haul.

As you're working The Amazing 30 Day Challenge, you may have days at the beginning when you're feeling a little fragile or a little down because you're stressed or tired, or maybe you're just still not buying into the notion that you have the power to change your life. And this is why raising the level of trust and confidence you have in yourself is so important. There are many habits, practices and exercises that I suggest throughout the book that will build your confidence over time. But in the meantime, if you're mired in negative energy, it's affecting you in ways that are noticeable to other people. So one question to ask yourself is, "How do other people perceive me?" And I'm talking about first impressions. What are you saying to the world about yourself with your attire, posture, personal grooming and hygiene and your overall energy? When you're not at your most confident, these seemingly superficial things are easy to neglect. You think, why bother? But that is a big mistake.

It starts, again, with the breath. Before you go out in public, if you're feeling a little anxious or down, you might want to do a few cycles of the breathing exercises from Chapter 3. On the final inhale, I want you to stand up, square your shoulders back and lengthen from your tailbone up through the crown of your head while relaxing the rest of the body. How do you feel? Good posture has been scientifically proven to enhance self-confidence, so not only are you projecting a look of confidence, you will actually start to feel more confident. Additional research conducted by social psychologist Amy Cuddy at Harvard Business School reveals that our first impressions are overwhelmingly based on how confident and trustworthy we deem a person to be. When you walk into a room you want to appear confident and approachable. If it feels awkward to walk around with a smile on your face, at least leave the mask of intensity at home and relax your facial muscles. And while there may be other things about your overall appearance you may want to change, your posture and facial expression are both things you can change immediately and will not cost you a thing.

When you're out in public, whether it's a social gathering, your workplace or a coffee shop, you have the opportunity to interact with other people. Even the prospect may get your heart palpitating and that annoying eye-twitch going. But not to worry! Remember in the chapter about breaking and establishing habits I talked about being mindful and prepared? It applies to stress-provoking situations and occasions that put your confidence to the test as well. For example, if you find it difficult to initiate a conversation, make sure you're on top of current events and have a few topics at the ready to use as icebreakers (but stay away from controversial subjects). Once the conversation gets rolling, make sure to make eye contact and speak up! Expressing an opinion, concurring with another's opinion or complimenting another's point of view or idea all say to the world that you are a self-assured individual. And making eye contact is a sign of respect in many Western cultures, and it lets the other person know that you are interested in what she has to say. I'm sure you've had the experience of having someone looking everywhere but at you during a conversation. How did that make you feel? Probably that the person was not really interested in getting to know you. Or maybe that they felt uneasy or a little intimidated. Quite the opposite of self-confident.

Complimenting others is another way to build your confidence when you're not feeling particularly compliment-worthy yourself. It is an act of generosity that makes both the giver and the receiver feel good. Think about how you felt the last time someone paid you a compliment. When you notice something about another person, it helps get you out of your own head and away from focus on yourself. The compliment can be about something superficial (as long as it's sincere), like something the person is wearing or a new hairstyle, or it could be an expression of admiration for an achievement or act of kindness. And the best part is you just might make that individual's day.

Another excellent way to affect self-confidence is to "dress the part." Of course we all want to ultimately be judged on who we are and not how we look, but we're talking about first impressions right now. And if you don't make a favorable first impression, other people will never give you the chance to show them how wonderful you are. This is something your mother probably told you when you wanted to dye your hair, get a tattoo or piercing, or were walking out the door in something she deemed risqué or somehow inappropriate. I know. I hate to agree with your mother, but she was right. People judge us on our appearance. I'm not saying you should change your personal style or become consumed with how you look. What I'm suggesting is that you take care to not appear as if you just rolled out of bed when you go out in public. Get rid of clothes that don't fit you properly, or at the very least, save your favorite sweats with the holes in the seat for nights at home. You don't need to go out and spend a lot of money on a new wardrobe or start contemplating plastic surgery. It all comes back to being attentive and acknowledging that little things, like how your pants fit, can make a huge difference in how you see yourself and how others see you.

Real Life: Bill

Bill is a very shy guy. When I first met him, he admitted being uncomfortable initiating conversations with anyone, let alone a woman. He sat on the edge of his seat as though he were afraid to fully occupy it, and generally avoided eye contact. Bill didn't give up any information voluntarily but with some gentle prodding on my part, he revealed he'd always been insecure, particularly around women he didn't know. But he wanted to date and was hoping to get into a long-term relationship in the future.

I coached Bill on eye contact. He blushed each time he made eye contact with me but kept working on it. I instructed him to focus on looking people in the eye — if it was a woman he was instructed to offer a brief smile. (He nearly fainted at the mere idea!)

A week later, he reported feeling more confident. "I know it's only eye contact, but it was really hard at first and I had to remind myself that it was a step I needed to take for myself. The smile was a little harder but then one woman gave me a big smile in return. I felt like a million bucks! That made it easier and it built me up."

Our next step was to initiate conversation — nothing major, just normal chitchat with cashiers, ticket takers, garage attendants. Bill found this step very hard at first, but just as he did with the eye contact, he persevered. He agreed to work on this assignment with women he was not attracted to ("just in case").

Once again, Bill reported positive results. "It's not like I had deep intellectual conversations with anyone, but they responded to me. It felt good." And soon he was confident enough to start complimenting others as well.

Bill's story demonstrates what is possible when we push ourselves to take small risks. He also worked on his posture and agreed to re-evaluate his wardrobe. Bill was clearly on his way to making great first impressions!

And a Little Exercise Never Hurt Anyone Either

Unless you've been living on a desert island since you arrived here on Earth, you are acutely aware that regular exercise is one of the keys to health and longevity. The benefits of physical activity for your body, brain and sense of well-being are well documented. Choosing a lifestyle that includes exercise has a positive cumulative effect on how you feel about yourself for many reasons. When you commit to a regular program of exercise, you experience a boost in self-confidence because you've set an intention and are following through. Whether it's playing tennis with a friend, waking early to go on a 30-minute walk before work or getting yourself to yoga class, when you push past your excuses and do it, that's a good feeling. Check that item off your list for the day! The great thing is, research shows that you don't have to spend hours in the gym each week: accumulate 150 minutes of moderate to vigorous physical activity per week, and you will reap many health benefits. Controlling your weight, and preventing or managing chronic health problems are the most obvious health benefits. But what about the psychological benefits? The immediate boons to your self-confidence that exercise promotes? And how can it affect other people's perceptions of you?

One study conducted by Professor Heather Hausenblas of the University of Florida demonstrated that simply the act of working out improves a person's self-image. In other words, after one exercise session, we think we look better even though there's no measureable improvement in fitness. Why is that? Depending on what you were doing, it could be you were genuinely enjoying yourself. Maybe you were working out with a friend or participating in something you had been looking forward to doing. So you feel happy and you exude that positive energy; others are drawn to that. The other mood enhancing qualities of moderate to intense exercise are due to the various brain chemicals that are stimulated, which contribute to feelings of relaxation and contentment. Even a 30-minute walk can produce a sense of calm and reduce anxiety. Now, if you want to lose weight in order to feel more confident in your body, you can do it in time if you commit to a lifestyle that includes regular exercise and a sensible healthy diet. But if you want to release some brain chemicals simply to feel more confident in your skin, you can do that today.

Amazing Life Habits

- *Find your voice and use it. Speak up, whether at work, home or in social situations. Contributing your thoughts and ideas to the conversation will help others get to know the real you and will build your confidence.*

- *Find a physical activity you enjoy and make it part of your daily/weekly routine.*

- *Take charge of your appearance and make the most of your assets.*

Daily Affirmation

I am worth knowing.

NOTES:

Chapter 6: My Self-Confidence Has Fallen

(and It Can't Get Up) - Comparing Yourself to Others

Sometimes nothing can burst your bubble of self-esteem more completely than a confident, good-looking person of the same sex. We've all experienced that moment. You're in a social situation, feeling pretty good about yourself, and then, boom! All attention is diverted in the direction of some beautiful interloper who strides in oozing confidence, warmth, graciousness, style, sex appeal, etc. (You can pick any quality that you're sure doesn't describe you.) Or maybe this person is similar in many ways to you; she just seems prettier and smarter. The person may even be an acquaintance or friend, not an interloper at all.

This is something I hear frequently in my practice, from both men and women. We often compare ourselves to other members of our sex, and 99.9% of the time, it's not favorably. For example, guys, if you see another man who has a thick shiny head of hair, and you've shaved your head to compensate for the fact that yours is thinning, you're not thinking, "I'm just as good-looking as he is. And I've got a great personality to boot!" Nope. What you're probably thinking is, "I wish I had that guy's hair. He's probably having more sex than I am." And even if you have a partner who reassures you that your bald pate is sexy, you see it for the lie it is the instant you catch her glancing at a man who is well endowed in the hair department.

I say this with compassion and understanding: Knock it off.

I know that's easier said than done, but the reality is, there are always going to be people who are "better" than we are in our eyes. And the only way that comparing yourself to those people is going to be productive is if you use them to inspire you. If that comparison motivates you to be the best you can be or to emulate their desirable quality in some way, that can actually be a buoy to self-esteem. If your neighbor, who has a great physique, frequently does yard work shirtless to show off his six-pack, and you think, "Man, I could never get in that kind of shape," you never will. But if you see your neighbor and think, "If he can do it, I can do it. I'm going to ask him what his workout regimen is," or "I'm going to finally join the gym," that's a great way to head off negative self-talk and set the bar high for yourself. Or let's say there's a woman in your office that everyone regards as a style maven. She always looks polished and put together, and it just seems to come effortlessly. Instead of putting yourself down and feeling frumpy whenever she's around, why not compliment her on her sense of style and find out what her secret is. Where does she shop, what does she read? It's always good to have a mentor in areas of our lives where our knowledge or skills are lacking.

Now, there are times when we do compare ourselves favorably to other people — at their expense. We might see another woman and think or say to friend, "She doesn't even dress her age!" or "What was she thinking when she put on that make-up?" So, yes, while we may feel superior by putting the other woman down, it's our insecurity talking. Women, especially, can be ruthless critics when it comes to other woman, especially when we're in a group. We judge, we pronounce, we stereotype. We do it because we feel threatened or are feeling so insecure that we have to lift ourselves up by comparing ourselves to someone who really doesn't have it together. And deep down, we fear that people may be saying the same things about us.

Real Life: Ming

Ming came to my office because he wanted to know how to increase his self-esteem. "Everyone I know has a great life. They're all so happy, have good friends, always going to great places. Me? I just work." My ears had perked up, "Really? Everyone you know?"

He nodded. "I see it all the time on Facebook or read it on Twitter. People post pictures of exciting vacations and important events they attend, interesting things they're doing in the community, shots of their adorable children. Just yesterday a friend's status pronounced, 'A big shout out to the world's best husband!' I read these things and I feel like my life isn't even worth mentioning."

Welcome to FOMO, or Fear of Missing Out. You probably know the feeling even if you don't know the term. It's the itchy fingers, that apprehensive feeling that you'll be hopelessly out of the loop if you're not constantly checking your Twitter feed or renewing your Facebook page. And there it is: Proof. Proof that everyone's life is better than yours. Everyone is on vacation, has the most amazing partner/spouse/kids/parents/siblings/job...

Want to know a secret?

They don't.

Most people post what's good and leave out the rest. That crappy day when the boss yelled at her? Not posted. That day when he discovered his wife was let go from her job and they're already sinking into debt? Not tweeted. And while it's true that lots of people post a range of experiences, if you're comparing your real life to their Facebook lives, you will typically hone in on the "my life is better than yours" postings.

Ming had himself convinced that everyone else was happier than he was and concluded he must suffer from low self-esteem. However, in sharing the details of his life, Ming described what sounded to me to be a pretty rich and fulfilling life. He was readily able to list things he liked about himself and seemed generally accepting of who he was. We explored when his feelings of 'less than' came up and, sure enough, it was when he was on social media.

Ming agreed to do a digital detox — a 48-hour period in which he was to refrain from checking any of his social media sites. He could check his email but that was it. No Facebook, no Twitter, no going to any site where people could post and comment about their lives.

Ming came in the next week and reported that those 48 hours had been difficult. "For one, I must spend a lot more time on those sites than I realized because it seems like all I thought about! Two, I kept wondering what I was missing out on. I finally asked my girlfriend to help me by going with me to the street fair. Then I kept thinking, 'Oh I should post this on Facebook because it's so funny!' But once I got back online after the 48-hours was up, I started feeling a little depressed when I started catching up on everyone's statuses and seeing everything I had missed out on. Then it dawned on me: I was upset about missing out … on other people's lives! I had just gone out and had a great time in the real world with my girlfriend, and at the time it didn't matter to me what anyone else was doing or what anyone else might think of what I was doing. It really made me start to wonder why I spent so much time comparing my life to the lives of my friends, whether true friends or Facebook 'friends'."

I asked Ming if he was willing to go a step further: a week without social media, which would also include a ban on texting. The only interactions he could have with friends and colleagues were to be in person or on the phone. He was dubious but agreed.

After the week was up, Ming came to a realization. "Okay, I see I don't have self-esteem issues, I have comparison issues!" He described talking to friends he regularly saw on social media and hearing from them that they indeed had ups and downs, they just didn't post them. "Your point is well-taken. We all have ups and downs, and if I focus on what I think I don't have, I will feel badly about myself. From now on, when I start worrying that my life is less than others, I will know I need to take another digital detox." I heartily agreed and suggested that a monthly digital detox of 2–7 days (the longer the better!) would help him keep things in perspective.

To all of you out there who tend to get sucked into the vortex of social media, remember the words of Michael Corleone from The Godfather, Part III, "Just when I thought I was out, they pull me back in." If you do a digital detox, don't just revert to the old habits in which you succumb to the siren song of Facebook the moment your fast is over. Work on having a balanced relationship with social media. Don't log onto your Facebook account or check Twitter the second you get bored. (By the way, it's okay to be bored once in awhile!) I'm not saying all social media is negative; there are many good things that have come from people being able to connect in this way. Only you know if you have a toxic relationship with these networking sites. If they leave you feeling badly about yourself and your life, if you spend more time following other people's lives than living your own, then it's probably time to seriously examine your online social activities.

Even though Ming's comparisons revolved more around lifestyle and social status, for many men, appearance and body image are areas of insecurity, just as they are with women. And in the past 40 years or so, men's dissatisfaction with their bodies has risen dramatically. Insecurities about sex appeal (women) and sexual potency (men) are also common complaints. But by and large, women are more likely to lack confidence when it comes to appearance and the stability of romantic relationships then men, and men are more apt to be anxious when it comes to economic status and career advancement. Economist and philosopher John Stuart Mill famously observed, "Men do not desire to be rich, but to be richer than other men." So what is the average Joe or Jill supposed to do in the face of the constant onslaught to our egos by the so-called best and the brightest of this world?

First of all, you become aware of when you're comparing yourself to someone else and you stop yourself right in your tracks. You've spent enough of your life comparing yourself to other people and feeling like you don't measure up. It's time to move on. And you start by rebalancing the equation with values in your favor. Remind yourself that no one's cornered the market on attractiveness: you're attractive too! You're good at your job — in fact, you just got a promotion. You're known throughout the neighborhood as the grill master for your aplomb with smoked meats, and you've been told you're a great storyteller — you've got some enviable qualities. This would also be a good time to repeat an affirmation such as "I have a lot to offer the world" to yourself. This is how you build confidence in yourself and work towards that emotional place where your rival can be herself, you can be yourself and what other people think about you doesn't really matter. Listen to constructive criticism and learn if there's something of use to you. But remember, just because someone has an opinion about you doesn't mean you're obliged to listen to it.

Amazing Life Habits

- *Keep a gratitude journal. List 2–3 things daily for which you are grateful.*

- *Do a 2- to 7-day digital detox at least once per month. Remember, there was a time not too long ago when we all survived without Facebook, Twitter, Pinterest, Tumblr, or Instagram.*

- *Look at others' admirable or enviable qualities as inspiration rather than condemnation of yourself. If you do find yourself comparing yourself negatively, stop and remind yourself of your positive attributes.*

Daily Affirmation

I am a strong and empowered person.

NOTES:

Chapter 7: Stick with Me Kid,

(We'll Go Places) - Listening to Your Inner Compass

When you were a child, you were probably more connected to your inner compass than you have been at any point since. "The mind of the beginner is empty, free of the habits of the expert, ready to accept, to doubt, and open to all the possibilities," according to Zen master Shunryu Suzuki. As we move through this life, picking up inhibitions and internalizing other people's expectations and judgments of us, we start to drift away from this inner compass. We may find ourselves straying down the wrong path and doing things that separate us from who we really are. Call it intuition, your internal wisdom or your "gut," but essentially it's that feeling of being grounded and having complete trust in yourself in the moment. Maybe you're thinking, "My inner compass must be defective, because I have never felt that kind of certainty with myself or my choices." But if you really think hard, I bet you can remember a time when you it spoke to you, even if it was a whisper. So often, we ignore that guiding voice that says, "Trust me. I don't know how I know, I just know." I think it's time to reconnect with your internal guide and start listening to what it has to say.

So what else can your inner compass do for you? Well, when you want to make positive changes in your life, it can be your best friend. It keeps you from reverting to old ways of negative thinking by silencing the voice that tells you, "I knew this wouldn't last," or, "You're too weak to change." It can save your life in certain situations or it can give you a new lease on life, as was the case with Sheila. She listened to her inner compass, which led her to follow her passion.

Real Life: Sheila

The first time Sheila walked in to my office, she told me matter-of-factly, "I've had years of therapy, and I'm not sure what you can do for me." One of the things I know after years of counseling hundreds of people is that when it come to making real changes in your life, thoughtful guidance and insight by a trained therapist is important, but timing is everything. The person sitting on my couch has to be ready to make a change, and it may take years for them to come to that point. In some cases, the individual may never be willing to give up familiar ways of living and being, no matter how destructive, for the unknown. For Sheila to declare, "I'm not sure what you can do for me," was very telling. It is my role to help facilitate self-awareness and growth, and offer insight, but in the end, Sheila had to be ready to listen to her inner compass and do for herself.

She reported doing very well financially in her profession, being in a comfortable relationship, and not having money concerns. "I have it all, so why am I not happy?" she lamented.

What we soon uncovered was that her current job, while paying a good salary, was not her heart's desire. It was her parents' choice for her, and they had incentivized her by paying for her education. Each time she reached a milestone in her education and later, her career, her parents rewarded her monetarily. She daydreamed about walking away from her job and following her life's passion in an unrelated field. As I listened to the excitement and yearning in her voice when she spoke of this, I asked her what she thought was stopping her from pursuing what sounded to me like her true vocation.

"I can't disappoint my parents, they would be so hurt and so angry. They would feel they'd wasted all that money on my education. Plus, you know my brother has been in and out of rehab for drug addiction, so it feels like it's my responsibility to be the child they can be proud of, someone to brag about to the relatives."

Sheila's compass was clearly pointing her to her heart's desire. But, she foresaw the potential for disappointing others, failing to live up to others' expectations, and hurt and anger. We worked on imagining different scenarios and different outcomes, and I asked her if she was prepared to accept the fallout if the reaction was negative. Once she was at peace with the decision to reveal her feelings to her parents, I reminded her one possible outcome might be that they would realize her happiness was the most important thing to them and even though they might not agree with her choice, they would support her.

When your fear of the negative reactions of others dictates your life choices, it's important to step back and regain some perspective. If you want to make a change in your life that will impact other people in some way, play out all possible scenarios in your head, not just the negative ones. Don't always assume you know how someone else will react because in doing so, you take away their autonomy and do them a disservice. We can have valid expectations of how people will behave based on observations and past experience. However, it is often a mistake to allow expectations to be a foregone conclusion. Once your brain accepts that there are multiple possible outcomes, your fear and resistance are lessened. You can imagine approaching the situation more calmly and with more confidence. This doesn't mean that others will always be happy with your decisions, but they will have to face the fact that you have a mind and will of your own and your decisions are yours and yours alone to make.

Sheila was met with an unexpected deadline in her deliberations about staying the course or listening to her heart. At the arts supply store she frequented, the owner told her he was retiring and hoping to sell his shop. It was an opportunity she felt she couldn't pass up, but she wavered about taking the risk. She had the support of her husband but she still feared disappointing her parents.

After asking her to close her eyes, I led Sheila through a visualization exercise in which she imagined herself in the shop on her first day as the new owner. She beamed. I asked her to envision her parents coming in and exclaiming over her good choice. I then had her imagine walking past the shop after someone else purchased it, and her face fell. Her eyes opened and she said, "That's it. I have to do this for me. This is my dream. My parents have already lived their lives, and it's time I lived mine. I'm going to do it!"

Several weeks later, Sheila came in holding a ring of keys. "It's mine! I told my parents how unhappy I have been in my current field of work and that I wanted to buy this shop. My dad said some mean things, but it seemed like my mom got it. My dad called me the next day and told me he loved me and wanted me to be happy. He even offered to help out if I needed anything! I am so happy!"

The sad truth is many people don't trust themselves to go after what they really want. Or they stop themselves for fear of failure rather than letting passion and interest be their guide. I've worked with many clients who engage in paradoxical thinking, such as "I really want to do well on this test but I'm not going to study tonight because that way, if I don't get a good grade, I can always tell myself it was because I didn't study enough." Or, maybe this sounds familiar to you? "I've loved writing since I was a kid but there's no way I'd ever be good enough to get anywhere with it, so why bother?"

Imagine how good it would feel for the student to study hard and have it pay off. Or what if the person wanting to write let himself write — for the pleasure of it, not because it had to be a job. If you know what interests you, if you know what nourishes your psyche, isn't it time to do something about it?

On the flip side, you should take action if you know when something or someone makes you feel bad, uncomfortable, or in extreme cases, fearful. Your inner compass is pretty reliable when it comes to reading people and situations but often, if you're like most of us, you dismiss it. Because you think you're overreacting. Or you don't want to offend or hurt someone's feelings — this is especially true of women. When it comes to people, you may not be able to articulate what it is that just doesn't sit right with you, but you know you feel worse about yourself or generally uneasy after interacting with that person. Some types of abuse are obvious while others are not, but if your inner voice is trying to tell you something, pay attention. Talk it over with a friend or a professional to see if you need to set limits or find a way out.

Amazing Life Habit

- *Check in with your inner compass first thing in the morning and set an intention for the day.*

- *Follow your passion and see where it leads. Some of the world's greatest achievements were manifested by dreamers who married passion with skill and old-fashioned hard work.*

- *Keep a "Curiosity List." Whenever you think of something you'd like to do or learn more about, write it down.*

Daily Affirmation

I am stronger and more confident when I listen to my inner compass.

NOTES:

Chapter 8: No Regrets

Trusting Yourself to Make Good Decisions

"Choice is the only tool we have that enables us to go from who we are today to who we want to be tomorrow," according to Dr. Sheena Iyengar, a professor at Columbia University and a respected authority on choice. Chew on that for a moment. Dr. Iyengar further asserts that we make approximately 70 conscious decisions every day. If you're coming from a glass-half-empty perspective, that seems like an awful lot of opportunities to mess up, right? But you're shifting away from that negative mindset and in your new worldview, I hope you see it as numerous chances to get things right. It does sound like an enormous amount of pressure. But think about it: with all those choices comes a great deal of freedom and power. Let's be honest, most decisions we make are pretty mundane. However, the cumulative effect of little decisions can be big. For example, if you decide to skip the Venti Vanilla Latte one morning, you'll save yourself from 320 calories and a whopping 44 grams of sugar. What if you did that four days per week and made the latte a treat on Fridays instead of your norm? Or let's say you decide to bite your tongue the next time your nosy co-worker tries to bait you into sharing some gossip. Perhaps you put the kibosh on the urge to buy yourself the latest iPhone and instead put that money in the bank. With time and consistency, these seemingly inconsequential decisions can reshape your mindset, your habits and your values and ultimately, your life.

In the process of creating an amazing life, you will make good and bad decisions. Of course, we'd all prefer to avoid making the bad ones, but if we weren't lugging around a suitcase or two filled with our bad choices, we wouldn't be human. While the consequences for our bad choices may range from mild embarrassment to financial loss, a police record or worse, the only thing we can do once the decision has been made is learn from it, do damage control, if necessary, and move on. Mistakes in judgment can provide opportunities for growth, boost our resiliency, build character and help develop coping skills. But this can only occur when we are willing to accept responsibility, open to the lesson to be learned and committed to history not repeating itself. That is the best-case scenario.

The consequences of bad decisions also have the power to destroy us mentally and emotionally, if we let them. And a string of bad decisions, for example, can stir up that negative self-talk and deliver a deafening blow to our self-esteem; in the most extreme instances, they can be life changing. But this doesn't mean you're cursed or doomed to a life created by your pathologically bad decisions. It means that maybe you just don't have the skills needed to make good decisions. Life will always present you with forks in the road and opportunities that require you to take action. The options can be as monumental as getting married to deciding whether or not to take a vacation. You don't have to analyze every little decision you make in a day. But the bigger ones deserve your time, attention and careful consideration.

Below are seven steps to help you make sound decisions. Some decisions require you to think on your feet, and you may not have the time for "careful consideration." These are the times when your inner compass and an internalized skill set can work together. For although haste may be preferable to accuracy in such situations, if you have practiced the skills of good decision-making and have anticipated instances in which you might be pressured to make a snap decision, you will be able to think faster and more clearly in the moment. But be on the alert for people trying to fabricate a sense of urgency. In most instances, save matters of life and death, you should have time enough to deliberate and make a thoughtful decision.

1. Identify: Pinpoint the decision to be made.

This can be trickier than it first seems. For example, let's say you have wanted to go back to school to get your graduate degree for some time. You have a full-time job, plus you have personal obligations to consider. Is the decision about you pursuing a passion, despite the inconvenience it may cause for others in your life? Or is it about taking that necessary next step to advance your career? Is it more of a financial decision — is this something your budget allows at this time?

2. Fact-find: Gather as much information as you can to assess your options.

Research potential universities and request admission information, such as academic requirements, tuition and other fees, and whether or not the school accommodates students who are employed full-time. Consider talking to your employer about a flexible schedule if needed. If you have other responsibilities outside of work, investigate options for delegating those responsibilities or discontinuing them for the time being (e.g. childcare arrangements, volunteer duties, regularly scheduled appointments).

3. Brainstorm: Review all of the information you've collected and come up with as many options as possible.

After doing your research, you've narrowed it down to two schools for which you would meet the admission requirements. Your boss is willing to offer you a flexible schedule on Tuesdays and Thursdays, which includes working from home. One of the schools has the classes you want on those days, but it's an hour drive from your house. The other school is on your way home from work but doesn't have the class schedule that's compatible with working full-time; you'd have to take night classes.

Determine which options are most compatible with your values and current life situation.

4. Assess values: Weigh the probabilities or possible outcomes.

In other words, what's the worst that can happen? Imagine the consequences of putting off school to a later date. Imagine choosing one school over the other. If you're afraid putting off your graduate degree much longer will ensure that you won't ever obtain it, and that you'll be stuck in the same job at the same salary for the rest of your working life, maybe it comes down to a decision between schools. What if you choose your first pick but then realize the commute is affecting your quality of life (and your car is ten years old!)? What if you can't keep up with your work responsibilities with the added pressure and time commitment to school?

5. Make a list: Write down the pros and cons in order of importance.

Sometimes when you compare the pros and cons side by side, your answer is staring you in the face. For example, pros for going with your second choice may be convenience and cheaper tuition. Cons may include getting behind at work or not being able to complete your degree as fast because you're limited to taking night classes.

6. Solicit opinions: If you're still unsure, consult a third party.

An objective pair of eyes on your dilemma can be helpful, only if you're already leaning in one direction. Because once you open the floor, you'll likely be presented with a variety of opinions that may make you feel even more conflicted. And be very wary of consulting anyone who has a vested interest in the outcome. In our back-to-school scenario, perhaps you and a friend who has been passed over for promotions at work have both talked about going back to school. If it's not a good time for him personally or financially to return to school, he may try to discourage you. My advice: get your guidance from another person whom you trust or who has been in a similar position. There may be some aspects about your decision that you haven't thought through or you may get feedback reinforcing your own viewpoint.

7. Make your decision.

You've done you're due diligence, examined your choices from every angle and taken what your inner voice is telling you under consideration. What's your decision? Pay attention to how you feel. Hesitation is not the feeling you're looking for. Uncertainty is no good. Relief's a good one. Confidence and pride are both emotions that confirm you've made a good decision for yourself. If you decide to enroll for the upcoming semester at your first choice, maybe there are some public transportation options that would allow you to be productive during your commute. If you decide to postpone school for a semester, you may be disappointed, but use the time to get things in order to ensure your success. Plus, if you go ahead and apply for the following semester and pay the various fees, you're less likely to talk yourself out of it, as you feared you might do if you waited much longer. And who knows? Maybe this will be the inspiration your friend needs to make the decision to return to school and you can encourage each other.

Real Life: Michael

Michael had a dilemma. One of his best friends was having a destination wedding, and he was debating whether or not he should he go. He wanted to be there for his friend, but the fact that he had recently declared bankruptcy complicated matters and made the decision more about financial responsibility then being a good friend.

"At this point, I know I can go without creating more debt. It would just mean delaying payment of my financial obligations resulting from the bankruptcy by a couple of months."

Michael was clearly torn. His relationship with his friend seemed to outweigh his commitment to his debt repayment plan. We brainstormed about other ways he might be able to set aside money specifically for the wedding trip. As the discussion progressed, Michael shook his head, "I really made a lot of bad decisions before and this seems to fall into that category. I want to go, so I'm trying to make it work. But in reality, it doesn't work at all."

Michael decided against the trip. When he talked to his friend, he was met with kindness and understanding. His friend preferred that Michael take care of his obligations, and they agreed to meet up for a celebratory dinner after the wedding. Though he was disappointed, he was confident he had made the right decision, "I know I did the right thing. I feel proud of myself for not getting carried away by my emotions."

Amazing Life Habits

- *Examine big decisions from more than one perspective.*

- *For every decision you make, consider both the long-term and short-term consequences.*

- *Consult with someone you trust when you are uncertain about a decision.*

Daily Affirmation

I am able to make decisions that benefit my life now and in the future.

NOTES:

Chapter 9: Learn Your Communication ABCs

Attend, Balance, Convey

Do you know what one of the most utilized yet underdeveloped communication skills is? It's listening. There's a reason we have two ears and only one mouth. According to studies, 45%-50% of our communication activities are spent listening. It's a critical skill for building and maintaining relationships, and you'd think we'd be better at it. Except for this: we're easily distracted. By the piece of spinach caught in the person's teeth, by thoughts of what we need to do when he finally finishes his story, or something completely random. Like wishing you'd cleared your computer history before you left the house. What if you were in an accident and someone had to go to your house to find some personal information and discovers you had been searching for "Sexy Halloween Costumes for Cats"?

Blame it on the monkey mind, boredom or our nonstop modern day lives. Whatever it is, you never want to hear the sentence, "Have you heard a word I've said?" Awkward! And complicating things further is the fact that men and women listen differently. If you've ever had a conversation with the opposite sex, this will not be news to you.

If you think you're a great communicator, feel free to skip this chapter. Though I should point out that most of us overrate our skills in this area. So maybe you are generally a good communicator, but there's this one person you just can't get through to, and it drives you crazy. Or perhaps people accuse you of being too critical, but as far as you're concerned, you're just being a good friend and telling them what they need to hear. Read on, you may find some useful tidbits.

There are a few basic skills that I call the Communication ABCs. Get these skills down and you can improve any relationship, whether it be personal or business. It all starts with what I opened the chapter with: listening.

A is for Attend

When we attend to someone we are caring for and paying attention to that person. In the most basic sense, we are present for that person. That is the essence of listening. In their book, Why Good Things Happen to Good People, Dr. Stephen Post and Jill Niemark devote an entire chapter to listening. In it, they cite psychoanalyst Theodor Reik who spoke of "listening with your third ear," which picks up on things unspoken. They write, "When we truly absorb another's story, we are saying, 'You count. Your life and feelings and thoughts matter to me. And I want to know who you really are.' We all crave just this — opening out from our solitude."

The idea of listening with your third ear is about learning to read what's going on below the surface with people. It's picking up on those cues of intonation, body language and energy to decipher the meaning behind the words. This is not Mind-Reading 101, it's being an empathic or active listener, not just giving "ear service" to the conversation. And when you do that you may start to learn some interesting things about yourself too. Maybe you'll discover that, yes, you do tend to interrupt others because you want to get your opinion on the record. Or maybe you realize you do tend to jump the gun and blurt out something irrelevant because you assume you know what that person is going to say next. As a result, your interactions and responses will be more thoughtful and authentic.

When you can put yourself in someone else's position and listen to them with your mind and your heart, that is when you make those magical connections that are what life is all about. Think about what it feels like to be acknowledged in that way. To feel respected like that. Every once in while, we all just need to shut up and take notice #getoveryourself. And I mean that in the nicest way possible.

B is for Balance

When someone tells you something or does something that you have an opinion about, it's hard not to state that opinion as clearly as possible. However, depending upon whom you're talking to, what the subject is and your delivery, you may find yourself on shaky ground. And keep in mind that you may be basing your opinion on limited information. It's important to balance what you really want to say against how the other person will receive it. I am not advising you to stay silent, just to temper the intensity of your message. Be tactful and respectful, not confrontational or self-righteous. Be curious about why the person feels or does as she does rather than judgmental. This can be difficult because sometimes we strongly disagree with our friends', partner's or family members' choices. And we don't want them to embarrass themselves or have something worse happen as a result of what we deem to be a poor choice. In that same spirit of balance, we also need to look at our motives for making our honest opinion known. Do we want to put ourselves in a more dominant position in the relationship or assume the expert role? Or perhaps we are the ones who will be embarrassed, not the other person. Food for thought.

In every relationship, you need to pick your battles. Sometimes it's better not to say anything unless you're asked for your opinion. When you are asked, the rules above still apply. You cannot justify hurting someone's feelings "for his own good." That's an all-expense paid ticket to Ass Town and an excellent way to sabotage your relationship and in fact, do irreparable damage over time. (There actually is a town in the Ukraine called Ass; you probably wouldn't want to go there either.) So for example, if your good friend, clearly delighted with her recent clothing purchase, asks you what you think about her new threads, pause to consider before you answer. Instead of telling her what you really think (the Eighties called and want their harem pants back), weigh the cost of her deflated ego against your need to call out others' fashion faux pas and respond accordingly. You might say, "That outfit isn't my style, but you obviously feel good in it, and that's all that matters." Then just let it be.

Speaking of style choices, I'm reminded of a couple I once counseled whose communication was out of balance. The husband had gone out on his own and purchased what he thought were some pretty funky, fashionable sneakers. His wife took one look and actually said, "I don't think so. Those are horrible." This was obviously not a balanced or respectful response and, not surprisingly, he became very defensive. She made things even worse when she said, "Do you want me to take you shoe shopping?" That remark completely shut him down. She justified the insult with, "I'm just telling you this for your own good." But what he heard was, "I know best." It recast their relationship more as parent/child child rather than two loving, equal partners.

If she had stopped to consider his feelings and given equal weight to his ego and her need to express her opinion, the scene would have gone very differently. In this case, she would have been better off going with, "Those shoes aren't what I would have picked for you, but you like them, and that's all that matters."

C is for Convey

Human relationships are complicated and sometimes it seems that no matter what we say, it's the wrong thing. But communication is an art you can become proficient in by utilizing your imagination and certain learnable skills. Conveying your message is the trickiest skill in this curriculum. If I give you only one piece of advice here, it would be to be mindful rather than mindless in the way you express yourself. This is what I was getting at when I talked earlier about balance and weighing your feelings against the feelings of the other person. Especially when you're asking someone to change a behavior. The art is all in the delivery.

Imagine how differently you would react if I said to you, "I'm sick and tired of picking up after you all the time! You'd think we lived in a barn!" versus, "It would really help me out if you'd pitch in a little more around here. Those socks have been lying there since yesterday. Would you mind throwing them in the hamper?" You might pick up the socks either way, but how likely are you to leave them on the floor again? I would say, highly likely, if I took the approach in the first example. No one likes to be nagged, berated or addressed in a disrespectful way. It immediately puts the person on the defensive. You're probably thinking, "But I shouldn't have to keep asking someone to do what she already knows she should be doing! It's obvious to me, why isn't it obvious to her?" I hear you. And it's hard to hide your frustration when you're confronted with the same irritating behavior over and over again. But the socks are still on the floor, right? You know that old saying, "You can catch more flies with honey than vinegar?" Couldn't hurt to give it a try.

Real Life: Diana and Devon

Diana and Devon had been together seven years when they first sought counseling. They agreed that their relationship suffered from communication breakdown. Frequently, according to Devon, seemingly small issues led to big disagreements. I asked if they thought they were essentially having the same argument over and over. They both nodded.

Diana's chief complaint was that Devon never listened to her. "He appears to be listening, but later he'll say something that indicates he wasn't listening at all!" Devon defended himself by saying he had a poor memory.

In situations like this, I'm inclined to believe Devon thought he was listening, but in reality he was only hearing

Diana. And most likely, from the way Diana described their interactions, he probably was tuning out at some point and not even hearing everything she was sharing with him. I suggested a nightly exercise during which they would practice listening to each other for a specified amount of time and then reflect back the other's words verbatim. This is an important element: no creative interpretation, improvisation or defending yourself (if the topic happens to be about you) allowed. Diana would talk about a topic of her choice for no more than two minutes while Devon devoted himself to listening to her. After Diana finished, Devon's task was to repeat back to her what she said in as much detail as possible, then ask her if he got it right. Then they would switch roles. The exercise is meant to focus both parties and slow communication down.

When they arrived for their appointment the following week, I asked how the communication experiment had gone. "I felt listened to, really listened to!" Diana exclaimed. "But I also realized I was unloading a lot of details on him and then getting mad when he didn't remember all of them. That's one thing I'm working on now." Devon affirmed that the exercise was helpful, but had a different realization. "I really thought I was listening, but the first couple of times I realized I only heard part of what she was saying before I got overwhelmed with the minutiae of her story. Once I focused my attention and really started listening to what she was saying because it was important to her, I found I was able to retain more of the information. I felt like it made a difference and that our relationship will be better going forward as a result of what we've learned."

No Bad-Mouthing Allowed

Alice Roosevelt Longworth, the sharp-tongued daughter of Theodore Roosevelt, famously kept a pillow on her settee embroidered with the words, "If you haven't got anything nice to say, come sit by me." Please don't be that person (and don't be the person who wants to listen to someone speaking unkindly about another, for that matter). When you tear down another person or spread malicious gossip, it really only makes you look bad. The gossip may be entertaining to be around in the short term, but that energy gets old quickly. Once people catch on that you're always talking about others or seem to delight in others' misfortunes, they're going to start to wonder if you're talking negatively about them behind their backs. This kind of behavior breeds mistrust and hurt feelings, and you don't want to be the source of that kind of negativity. Keeping mum about things that have been shared with you in confidence and not perpetuating rumors is a quality that people respect. And it will make you feel better about yourself. Instead of taking Alice Roosevelt Longworth's pillow to heart, why not follow the advice of a little animated rabbit: "If you can't say somethin' nice, don't say nothin' at all." Well said, Thumper.

Amazing Life Habits

- *Be a great listener.*

- *Don't say something behind someone's back that you wouldn't say to his face.*

- *Before telling someone something "for her own good," stop and consider how that person will receive the information.*

Daily Affirmation

I strengthen my relationships by being mindful in my personal interactions.

NOTES:

Chapter 10: You Think You've Had a Bad Day?

(Let me Tell You About Mine) Managing the Toxic People in Your Life

There is probably at least one person in your life that you try to avoid because you feel depressed or irritated after every interaction. You see her heading toward you out of the corner of your eye and quickly duck into the bathroom. You see his name come up on your cell phone and hit "ignore." Do you remember the Debbie Downer character portrayed by Rachel Dratch on Saturday Night Live? One of the reasons the sketches were so funny was because most of us do know someone like Debbie Downer. You're in a fine mood and then "wah wah wah," here comes the person you know is going to rain on your parade. These are what we call toxic people. They complain constantly, they're almost always critical or negative, and they never seem to have a kind word to say about anything or anyone. If something is going on in your life that you want to talk about, forget about it. Before you've gotten a word out, they've launched into their saga, "Well, let me tell you what happened to me today!" And then you're trapped for 30 minutes in a hail of negativity.

Emotionally draining — you may have heard them referred to as emotional vampires — and difficult to be around, toxic people are individuals who just take and take and take. It could be a friend, relation, or someone you work with, and in some cases, it's impossible to avoid them. But if there is somebody in your life that you dread being around and you come away from feeling depleted, you need to figure out how to mitigate their toxic effect on you one way or the other. Try the following steps to deal with the toxic people in your life.

The ANTIDOTE for Toxic People

Anticipate the Encounter

You can probably pretty accurately predict the way things will go when you see this person. You may not know exactly what they're going to complain about or criticize, but the tone will be generally consistent with what you know about this person. Let's say the next time you see your co-worker, Mike, he's griping about the horrible traffic again and how it's always horrible, etc. Often it's a good idea to defuse the person's negativity with a positive observation and then change the subject. So maybe your response to Mike could be, "Yeah, it can be irritating, but I guess it's the price we pay for living in such a great city! Hey, do you happen to have those monthly sales reports ready?" Usually toxic people have some consistent themes in their complaints. So if you can imagine the interaction ahead of time, you can develop a strategy for dealing with people like Mike and minimize their impact on you.

Narrow the Window of Time

Keep the discussion short and don't let yourself get dragged into the person's drama. Sometimes an effective way to do this is to refer the person to a third resource for a different perspective. Whatever it is that the toxic person in your life gets worked up about, you don't want to get into a lengthy debate, and you certainly don't want to be in a position where you can't get away. If your 50-something sister-in-law Ellen is constantly complaining about her back and every body ache and creak she has, you could refer her to a bodyworker, a physician or say something like, "You might want to check out Andrew Weil's book, Healthy Aging." While they're considering, you can smoothly slip away. If this doesn't work, change the subject.

Talk about the Weather

Stick to safe, non-controversial topics. Don't get into politics. Don't get into dating. Don't get into family dynamics or religion. Do not take whatever bait he's dangling in front of you. What's left? Well, there's music, books and sports, for example. A truly toxic person can be critical about almost anything, but these subjects will generally keep you out of dangerous territory. Or perhaps this person actually has a hobby he enjoys and always perks up when he talks about it. So you might say, "Hey Dave. Great weather this past weekend. Bet you were out on the golf course." Indulge him for a few minutes about his golf game and then be on your merry way.

Insulate Yourself

What toxic people are really looking for is emotional validation. They want your attention, your sympathy and in some cases, they may expect you to choose sides. Of course, you don't want to be completely dismissive or appear uncaring; you want to be a good friend or family member. But you can't let yourself get too emotionally invested in their stories. Keep in mind, you're hearing only one side. If it's obvious to your friend Anna that you're starting to follow her down the rabbit hole, she will just pull you in deeper. And it's hard not to express sympathy when she's going on about a situation in which someone has done her wrong. But you must keep things in perspective; you know Anna's modus operandi, and you've been down this road before where something you said came back to haunt you. You might say, "Well, that sounds like it was really hard for you," and let that be your final word. If you ask questions, you will prolong the conversation and indulge her desire to be a victim. Don't let yourself be the enabler in this dynamic.

Define Your Boundaries

This is so important when you're dealing with negative people. You need to establish your rules of engagement and learn how to say no. Toxic people can sense weakness. If you give in once, a toxic person will see that crack in your armor and exploit it. "He gave in last time, I bet I can get him to give in this time."

Own Your Emotions

You can't always control what happens to you; you can only control how you react to the things, or in this case, people, that happen to you. Take charge of your emotional well-being. What does this mean? Don't let an encounter with a negative person determine your mood. Shake it off. Leave it with them. If you can't do that and feel you need to say something, let them know you didn't appreciate a particular comment or felt it was inappropriate. Sometimes it's difficult not to take it personally, but remember, that's all on them. You take ownership of your well-being, and they can own their negativity.

Toss Out a Compliment

One thing that can stop a toxic person in her tracks is a compliment. You may recall we talked about the power of compliments in the earlier chapter on confidence. Everyone appreciates a sincere compliment, and if you deliver a well-timed compliment to a person in the middle of a negative rant, they simply won't know what to do. Now don't be fooled for a minute that toxic people aren't aware of how people react to them. They see that people avoid them, withdraw in conversation and don't seem to be listening attentively. And this feeds their insecurity. Their habit loop tells them they must complain more vociferously and play the victim role to the hilt in order to hold people's attention, even though this behavior repels others even more. When you notice something positive about a career complainer, it can change his whole attitude and demeanor. This can temporarily turn off a toxic person's negativity autopilot, give him a little hit of self-confidence and allow him to see a different reflection of himself. But again, the praise must come from an authentic and sincere place or he will see right through it.

End the Cycle of Negativity

The final step in dealing with toxic people is to not perpetuate the negativity. When you've had an encounter with a Debbie or Dave Downer, you can emerge feeling like you need to detoxify yourself somehow. You may be tempted to go vent to someone else about your encounter. "I can't believe she went on and on about this thing all over again. I've heard it so many times," you might complain to a friend. And then you are the negative person. If you need to detoxify, do something positive for yourself. Have a conversation with a person you know always makes you feel good. Get outside. But don't spread toxic waste.

Let's say, however, the toxic person (or persons) in your life is someone you see on a regular basis, sometimes for large amounts of time. If you have a close relationship with the person, the strategies above may only serve as stopgap measures. For example, if the toxic person happens to be a close friend or a relative you really care about, the best strategy may be to stage a one-on-one intervention when you're feeling strong and confident. You might begin with, "I enjoy our time together, but it feels to me that you're in a negative place right now and I leave our interactions feeling very drained. Is there something going on that I don't know about?" You showing genuine interest in their well-being may be what they need to break out of the cycle of negativity and show some vulnerability. Sometimes we shroud ourselves in negative energy as a self-protective trait — something that serves to keep people at arm's length. This could backfire, as the person may see it as an invitation to up her negativity game. But if it makes sense and you're willing to take the risk, addressing the issue head on could be the best thing for your relationship and can end the cycle of negativity for both of you.

Everybody Has One

The opinionator. You know the type. These people just can't seem to keep their opinions to themselves, bless their hearts. Though their style and methods can often feel intrusive, I would venture to say that, in most cases, their outspokenness on the subject of your life comes from a place of love. They want what's best for you...and they are certain they know what that is. But opinionators are tricky. Some of them really do believe they're being supportive by offering their (unsolicited) advice or opinion. But the others? Not so much. And they may not even realize the deceit themselves. Their reasons can be varied and many, from insecurity and jealousy to fear and ignorance. Everyone develops a point of view based on his history, experiences, values and beliefs. It doesn't mean their perspective is wrong, but we're talking about your life, and you may be making decisions about it based on a completely different set of criteria. Even though opinionators do not always fall into the category of "toxic people," they do need to be managed in much the same way. Using your Communication ABCs and the ANTIDOTE will help you greatly with these challenging relationships.

As I mentioned in Chapter 1, once you start making positive changes in your life, the opinionators will appear. And until you gain a foothold on the path to your amazing life, you need to be wary of those trying to lure you in a different direction or halt your progress altogether. And it's hard in the early stages because your inner compass is still trying to assert itself, and the voices of the opinionators are much louder and more convincing. You may think, "Well, he's got a point. Maybe what I'm doing isn't a good choice for me."

Real Life: Andrew

Andrew was determined to get into shape. When he finally came to see me, he professed that he was "sick and tired of being sick and tired." He outlined his plan for improving his physical health and overall well-being, which included attending a boot camp five mornings a week and buying pre-made meals from a local healthy foods kitchen. He felt optimistic for the first time in a long time that he could have a positive impact on his health.

When I talked to him a week later, he was having second thoughts. "My friend said she thought boot camps were a bad idea because they aren't tailored to the individual and the trainers push people too hard, sometimes to the point of injuring themselves. She also said that pre-made food is always unhealthy, that those places just charge more because they label it "health food," but that I can get the same stuff in the frozen section of the supermarket!" I asked if he had checked out the information with the boot camp trainer or inquired about the ingredients in the pre-made meals. He stated he had not and agreed to make some phone calls.

When he came in the following week, Andrew was excited. He told me he'd made the phone call to the trainer and felt very encouraged by her. He'd also inquired about the food and was impressed by the fact that the ingredients were locally sourced and used no preservatives. Andrew then reported with pride that when his friend had expressed her opinion yet again, he had responded to her by saying, "Mary, I appreciate your concern but this is my decision and I hope you will respect that. It would be great if you could just support me in my effort to take better care of myself."

You can't please everybody all of the time, and if you try, guess who's going to end up on the losing end? That's right, it's you. Don't give someone else's opinion or judgment more weight than your own. If it's coming from someone you love and respect, the best you can do is take their advice under consideration and try to view it as objectively as possible. But in the end, it's your opinion that matters. So you might go back to the person and say, "I see your point and appreciate where you're coming from, but I just don't see things the same way. You may be right, and I may regret this decision, but this is what I have to do for me." So you're not telling the person they're wrong, you're just respectfully disagreeing with their opinion on whatever the matter at hand is. And whether it's having to disagree with someone whom you know truly cares about you or it's shutting down an opinionator who uses intimidation and condescension as a way to make themselves feel superior, when you can stand up for yourself, it's an amazing feeling. And you now know the steps needed to make good decisions for yourself, so other people's opinions are by invitation only. And remember, you're creating the life you want to live, not the life they want you to live.

Amazing Life Habits

- *Defuse negativity with positivity.*

- *Limit your interactions with toxic people as much as you possibly can. Life is to short to be caught up in someone else's negative energy.*

- *Assert your right to respectfully disagree with other people when it comes to their opinions about your life. Consider the source and the intention before dismissing an opinion outright. Sometimes people just need to know what your boundaries are.*

Daily Affirmation

I surround myself with people who lift me up and accept me for who I am.

NOTES:

The Amazing 30 Day Challenge

Program Preparation

1. Choose your Amazing 30 Day Challenge start date and put it on your calendar

There's some prep work that needs to take place beforehand, so select a date 7-10 days in the future.

2. Create an Amazing 30 Day Challenge resource folder

If you already have a folder or notebook around the house, that will work just fine. If not, you can purchase one or if you prefer to record everything digitally, there are many apps out there that will fit the bill. Just make sure it's capable of storing inspirational or motivational material you may come across over the next 30 days. You might find something on the Internet, in a magazine or a book, so however you can organize this material most effectively so that you have easy access is all that matters. You'll also record any thoughts, observations or feelings that you have before, during and after the challenge.

3. Answer the questions posed in the Dial Dialogues™

I know you're ready to get started, but in order to set yourself up for success, it's important for you to become mindful of your current habits, check in with your inner compass and set your intentions. If you haven't already done so, please revisit the Dial Dialogues™ (found in the

Introduction) and answer the questions from parts 1-3. Before beginning the challenge, I recommend you observe for a minimum of 7 days how you're currently spending your time in order to have a baseline for comparison at the end.

4. Choose one major lifestyle change to focus on for the next 30 days

The Dial Dialogues™ are designed to help you identify what you truly want in your life. The fourth step in the process is to set a specific goal for yourself and to lay out a plan for achieving it. This will be the foundation of your Amazing 30 Day Challenge.

Knowing the life you want is within reach is thrilling prospect! You may have several goals to achieve and major changes in mind that you want to start working toward RIGHT NOW. Patience, Grasshopper. If you haven't been successful reaching your goals or making sustainable changes in your life up until this point, it may be that you've been overwhelmed. Once you started on that list of self-improvement to-dos, it snowballed into something you couldn't face and you just gave up before you saw any real results. Or maybe the sheer magnitude of your goal made it feel unobtainable. If you can get a handle on one aspect of your life, that can often have a positive effect on other areas. But the devil's in the details, so you've got to be very specific and break things down into manageable tasks. If other changes start to happen organically, that's wonderful! My point is, do not put so much pressure on yourself that you buckle before the 30 days are up. Taking on too much is one surefire formula for failure.

Now, if you don't believe me and decide to disregard my advice, all is not lost. If you find yourself struggling under the weight of too many self-renovation projects, simply step away from all but one and give that one your all for the rest of the 30 days. Once you feel comfortable with that change, go back and look at your list again. Maybe then you can reprioritize and then just start knocking out your goals, one by one, every 30 days.

Amazing Days 1-7

Remember that feeling of joyful anticipation you experienced before a holiday or your birthday when you were a kid? Setting a new course for yourself may conjure up similar emotions: a little apprehension, not knowing what exactly to expect, mixed with a feeling of excitement. Tamp down that apprehension and anxiety by reminding yourself why you are making this change a priority in your life. Sure, you may have tried before, but yesterday's attempts are not predictors of today's outcome!

Be prepared for your brain to try to find some loophole that will get you out of seeing the Challenge through to the end. You'll really need to closely monitor the autopilot switch and not allow it to be engaged. The Amazing 30

Day Challenge is not about willpower, it's about strategy. So the most important factors to your success will be planning, planning, planning!

The first seven days are the easiest for some while others find these early days the most difficult. Why the difference? Some people thrive on challenges but later become bored as a task becomes routine. Others struggle with making changes initially because it feels strange and uncomfortable but then relax as the new routine becomes more familiar. Figure out which camp you fall into and tailor your strategy accordingly.

Read: The notes you have made over the past week or so in preparation for the challenge. These notes reflect the "you" before The Amazing 30 Day Challenge. Now imagine the life you want to create. Project forward 30 days. This week is the beginning of something great.

Write: 5 things you like about yourself today

Watch*: Matthew Cutts: Try Something New for 30 Days

Shawn Achor: The Happy Secret to Better Work

Do: Eat a healthy breakfast

Hand out 3 compliments

Assess your wardrobe – donate items that no longer fit you (physically or figuratively!)

Practice an Amazing Life Habit: Get 7-9 hours of sleep each night.

*Note: All "Watch" assignments for The Amazing 30 Day Challenge can be accessed at www.ted.com.

Amazing Days 8-14

It's week two, and you are now creating a new habit. Keep up the forward momentum but also take the opportunity to reassess your first week. What obstacles did you encounter? If you stumbled or struggled, consider what those episodes taught you and cut yourself some slack. Change challenges us to use our brains differently. As you enter this second week, tweak your plan if needed and stick to it. You're doing it!

Read: A book, magazine or article that inspires you. Maybe it's a work of fiction by an author you particularly admire or a non-fiction book on a topic related to the changes you want to make in your life or a goal you're pursuing. Maybe you never have time anymore to read through the paper or The New Yorker anymore. Set aside time this week to do so.

Write: A thoughtful letter or e-mail to someone whom you haven't been in touch with for awhile. Let them know you've been thinking about them.

Watch: Candy Chang: Before I Die, I Want to …

Brené Brown: The Power of Vulnerability

Do: Volunteer your time somewhere this week. Volunteermatch.org is a great place to find ongoing volunteer opportunities.

Get outside around nature, weather permitting. If not, visit your local botanical garden or horticultural center.

Treat yourself to a pampering session. Maybe it's a manicure, massage or facial. It could be luxe (a nice spa) or luxe light (something you do at home). Local massage schools often offer clinics where students give massages as part of their training at more affordable rates than you'll find at a spa or salon.

Practice an Amazing Life Habit: Keep a "Curiosity List."

Amazing Days 14-21

Heading into week three, you should be feeling pretty good about yourself. But no resting on your laurels! Remember, this is The Amazing 30 Day Challenge, not The Amazing 14 Day Challenge. You should definitely give yourself credit for staying focused and making it to this point, but beware of your inner saboteur. The voice that says, "You've done great so far! You can cheat just this once — take a day off! You can get back with the program tomorrow." The brainpower supporting this new habit isn't quite strong enough to withstand even one day of cheating.

That way of thinking is a slippery slope for some people, so don't put yourself to the test. Keep on keepin' on!

Read: "35 Questions That Will Change Your Life" www.forbes.com/sites/jasonnazar/2013/09/05/35-questions-that-will-change-your-life

Write: Think of a recent positive interaction you had and describe how it came about. What happened and why was it positive. How did you feel afterwards? What did you learn from it?

Watch: Ron Gutman: The Hidden Power of Smiling

Amy Cuddy: Your Body Language Shapes Who You Are

Do: Buy an enhancement for your wardrobe that's within your budget.

Smile or wave at 3 strangers

Pay attention to your posture. No slumping this week!

Practice an Amazing Life Habit: Take charge of your appearance and make the most of your assets.

Amazing Days 21-30

You're in the home stretch! Stay vigilant — you've just got ten days to go. This is the part in the Challenge where you should start noticing some collateral benefits of pursuing your original goal or habit change. This ripple effect is not predictable or guaranteed, but when it happens, it can be the ultimate motivator to continue your good work beyond the 30 days and beyond your original goal. Be proud of the progress you've made thus far, and before you get out of bed in the morning, visualize yourself achieving the goals you've set for yourself. Imagine how you will feel on day 30. (Cue "Theme from Rocky") Sweet, right?

Read: (For Amazing Day 30) Your notes and answers to the questions from the Dial Dialogues before you started the challenge. How have things changed? How have you changed?

Write: 5 things you like about yourself today

Watch: Richard St. John: Success is a Continuous Journey

Andy Puddicombe: All It Takes Is 10 Minutes

Do: Choose a theme song. It may seem kind of corny, but I believe most people have theme songs, they just don't admit to it. Theme songs are great for motivation and inspiration. Play your theme song when you need a little extra encouragement to see you through these final challenge days and beyond.

Step out of your comfort zone. Do something you wouldn't have done four weeks ago.

Practice an Amazing Life Habit: Keep a gratitude journal

Feel proud of yourself!

What will be the next chapter in your Amazing Life?

Amazing Life Habits

1. Carve out time each week to do something you truly enjoy.

2. Get 7-9 hours of sleep each night.

3. Turn off electronic devices 30-60 minutes before turning in for the night.

4. Institute a daily 15-minute de-cluttering practice.

5. When you get the mail, deal with it immediately.

6. Clean out the inside of your car weekly, and consider treating her to a good wash every other month.

7. Take 10-15 minutes at the beginning or end of each day for a breathing meditation.

8. Take care of your lungs.

9. When confronted with a person or situation that stresses you out, take a moment to calm down with a few cycles of breathing exercises before speaking or acting.

10. Before trying to replace an old habit or establish a new one, identify possible obstacles to your success and create a plan to overcome them.

11. Drive a different route to or from work a few days per week.

12. Replace an unhealthy behavior with something healthy.

13. Find your voice and use it.

14. Find a physical activity you enjoy, and make it part of your daily/weekly routine.

15. Take charge of your appearance and make the most of your assets.

16. Keep a gratitude journal.

17. Do a 2 to 7day digital detox at least once per month.

18. Look at others' admirable or enviable qualities as inspiration rather than condemnation of yourself.

19. Check in with your inner compass first thing in the morning and set an intention for the day.

20. Follow your passion and see where it leads.

21. Keep a "Curiosity List."

22. Examine big decisions from more than one perspective.

23. For every decision you make, consider both the long-term and short-term consequences.

24. Consult with someone you trust when you are uncertain about a decision.

25. Be a great listener.

26. Don't say something behind someone's back that you wouldn't say to his face.

27. Before telling someone something "for her own good," stop and consider how that person will receive the information.

28. Defuse negativity with positivity.

29. Limit your interactions with toxic people as much as you possibly can.

30. Assert your right to respectfully disagree with other people when it comes to their opinions about your life.

31. Sign up to receive daily emails with motivational tips, support, and encouragement at www.TheAmazing30.com!

Daily Affirmations for an Amazing Life

- *I have the right to take time for myself to do things I enjoy.*

- *Physical clutter blocks the path to the life I want to live.*

- *With every full breath I collect positive energy and expel all discomfort and negativity.*

- *I feel strong and good about myself when I follow through on my intentions.*

- *I am worth knowing.*

- *I am a strong and empowered person.*

- *I am stronger and more confident when I listen to my inner compass.*

- *I am able to make decisions that benefit my life now and in the future.*

- *I strengthen my relationships by being mindful in my personal interactions.*

- *I surround myself with people who lift me up and accept me for who I am.*

References & Sources

Introduction

Gardner, Benjamin. "Busting the 21-Day Habit Formation Myth." 'Health Chatter:' The Health Behaviour Research Centre Blog. (June 29, 2012). Available online at http://blogs.ucl.ac.uk/hbrc/2012/06/29/busting-the-21-days-habit-formation-myth/

Hilgers, Lauren. "Meet the Man Who Built a 30-Story Building in 15 Days." (September 25, 2012). Available online at http://www.wired.com/design/2012/09/broad-sustainable-building-instant-skyscraper/

Plummer, William. "Jack Kerouac: The Beat Goes On." The New York Times. (December 30, 1979). Available online at http://www.nytimes.com/books/97/09/07/home/kerouac-plummer.html

Torgovnivk, Kate. "The Single Best Way to Lose Weight." (Retrieved August 28, 2013). Available online at http://www.goodhousekeeping.com/health/diet-plans/food-diary-diet-success-3.

Chapter 1

Czeisler, Charles A. "Perspective: Casting light on sleep
deficiency." Nature. (May 13, 2013). Available
online at
http://www.nature.com/nature/journal/v497/n7450_
supp/full/497S13a.html#auth-1

"Your Brain on Computers." Series of articles presented by
The New York Times. (June–November, 2010).
Available online at
http://topics.nytimes.com/top/features/timestopics/s
eries/your_brain_on_computers/index.html

Chapter 3

"Understanding the Stress Response." Harvard Health
Publications. (March 2011). Available online at
http://www.health.harvard.edu/newsletters/Harvard
_Mental_Health_Letter/2011/March/understanding-
the-stress-response

Chapter 4

Duhigg, Charles. The Power of Habit: Why We Do What
We Do in Life and Work. (New York: Random
House, 2012).

Chapter 5

Capps, Rob. "First Impressions: The Science of Meeting People." Wired. (November 20, 2012). Available online at http://www.wired.com/wiredscience/2012/11/amy-cuddy-first-impressions/

"Exercise Frequency May Not Matter As Long As You Work Out 150 Minutes A Week, Study Finds." Huffington Post (June 21, 2013). Available online at http://www.huffingtonpost.com/2013/06/21/exercise-frequency-150-minutes-metabolic-syndrome_n_3473873.html

"Just doing exercise convinces people they look better." The Telegraph (October 12, 2009). Available online at http://www.telegraph.co.uk/health/healthnews/6306524/Just-doing-exercise-convinces-people-they-look-better.html.

Chapter 7

Suzuki, Shunryu. Zen Mind, Beginner's Mind. (New York & Tokyo: Weatherhill, 2000).

Chapter 8

Tasler, Nick. "What Is Your Momentum Factor?" Strategic Thinking blog. Psychology Today. (August 30, 2012). Available online at http://www.psychologytoday.com/blog/strategic-thinking/201208/what-is-your-momentum-factor.

Chapter 9

Bambi. John Algar, Samuel Armstrong, et.al. Walt Disney Studios. 1942. Film

Mallon, Thomas. "Washingtonienne." The New York Times. (November 18, 2007). Available online at http://www.nytimes.com/2007/11/18/books/review/Mallon-t.html.

Post, Stephen P., and Jill Neimark. Why Good Things Happen to Good People. (New York: Broadway Books, 2007).

About the Author

Drema Dial, Ph.D., earned her doctoral degree in Counseling Psychology from The University of Texas at Austin and has established a reputation as a respected psychologist in the self-proclaimed "Music Capital of the World." Her professional associations include Texas Psychological Association, the International Red Cross, and the Equality Texas and Human Rights Campaign. She has also served on the Board of Trustees for the Texas Psychological Association and on the Board of Directors for The Wright Wellness House.

Dr. Dial has always been fascinated with human behavior and relationships, and the connection between one's past and present. This passion led her to the psychology profession and continues to guide her practice. Years of experience, education and training have made her a well-rounded psychologist, but her intuition and keen powers of observation are what allow her to help clients "in the moment." She believes when we can truly be present, reality becomes more alive and dynamic. Possibilities open up and the big picture can come together more easily.

For more tips from Dr. Dial and information on creating a life you want to live, visit www.TheAmazing30.com and http://www.askandgetclass.com.

Acknowledgements

Heartfelt thanks to the following people who helped incubate this into being: Erin Matlock for her early vision and support, Shelley Guerra who took this into her greatly skilled editor hands and helped make this a reality, my cover designer, Diana Ani Stokely, and my loving writers' group: Abriel Louise Young, Jan Morris, Nancy Kelly, Richard Holt, Lois Graham, and Robert Murphy.

Thanks also go to those who enthusiastically volunteered to read and provide feedback — you made a difference!

And, most importantly, my Judy, without whom I wouldn't have dared to dream so big.

www.ingramcontent.com/pod-product-compliance
Lightning Source LLC
Chambersburg PA
CBHW05203528052f6
45791CB00010B/2971

LATIN AMERICA: A QUEST FOR PEACE

The knot of our solitute

LUIS CHESNEY-LAWRENCE

2012

Oxford University
Project For Peace Studies
Award - 1884
(United Kingdom)

Oxford University
Project For Peace Studies Award 1984
(United Kingdom)

Universidad Central de Venezuela
Facultad de Humanidades
y Educación (UCV-FHE, 2009)

Consejo de Desarrollo Científico y
Humanístico (UCV-CDCH, 2009)
Proyecto No. PI-07-7277-2009

All works from CDCH are sumitted to referees

Eco - Ed Publications (NGO)

Luis Chesney Lawrence
Latin America: A Quest for Peace
The Knot of our Solitute
1st. edition, 2012

Design and assembly by Seraidi Chesney Sosa

ISBN-13: 978-1470089221
ISBN-10: 147008922X

Published by:

CONTENTS

REFERENCES

ABSTRACT

This book is concerned with Latin America and its history. It- is intended to reflect the main feature of the historical process of this area: the violence, and the continous aggression against the life and cultural forms of this continente To this end, the interpreting of peace in Latin America would be relevant the use of the concept of dependency as a basic category of structural condition of its society. Thus, three cases of study are presented to show three different forms of instability and violence in this continent: (1) The Spanish exploitation during the colonial period in the so called "white-gold" era of sugar, (2) The ffect of the liberal economic system during the XIXth Century in the so called "banana-republics" of Central America, and (3) The industrial dependency since the XXth Century, whose most prominent case is the oil extraction, the so called "black gold" ofVenezuela. This critical view is complemented by a previous section on the way of life of the indigenous populations before the discovery of America, and a final section concerning the present situation in the region.

INTRODUCTION

"Peace studies are concerned not only
with the means of preventing wars,
but with factors essential to a more
stable, more just and therefore more
peaceful world".
(Oxford University Project
For Peace Studies,1984)

Once, over four hundred years ago through the mistake of a
Genoese-Jew, America entered into history. By America, we
refer to that part of the world actually known as Latin America.
from that period in history, America or Latin America, as it has
continued to be named, lost the right to live in peace. This loss
was inflicted upon the peoples of the region "when
Renaissance Europeans ventured across the ocean and buried
their teeth in to the troats of the Indian civilizatios" (Galeano,
1979, p.3) Time has passed and yet the situation remains the
same.

Along this miserable way, we have even lost our
original name of Americans. This title is now used by the
citizens of the United States of America. Flourishing nations
such as the Haitians and Cubans were well established before
the "Mayflower" pilgrims of Plymouth arrived to settle in

America. But, from that period in history Latin America became a sub-America, a sort of second class group of nations with a diffuse identity.

However, our history is not only that of a fabulous kingdom, a wonderland shamed by the conquest, the gold or silver. We are actually a source of reserves of oil, of iron, of copper, of meat and raw materials. But, history repeats itsele in as much as the more wealth we gain the less peace we receive. Despite our natural resources we are also poor. Among more than 350 million Latin Americans, at least 15% are unemployed or underemployed, 30% are illiterate, 50% of the population is under eighteen years old, 40% are just children. Half of the people live in crowded impoverished conditions. The human murder by poverty is a secret war: every year, un-noticed by the world, three Hiroshima bomps explode over the continent, a continent once called the New World. This violence is increasing. George W. Ball (1983) stated that it is possible to act with impunity because the poor cannot begin a world war. Dwight D. Eisenhower prophesied that if the world's inhabitants continued multiplying, there would be the danger of revolution. That is the reason that the United States missions have sterilized thousands of women in Amazonia: it is more hygienic and effective to kill guerrillas in the womb than in the mountains ort he streets (Ibid, pp. 7-12).

When Christopher Columbus ventured across the sea in 1492, he had accepted the challenge of legends: terrible storms for his ships; fear of monsters, terror of sea serpents and the unknown. The world was then only the Mediterranean Sea with its uncertain horizons: Europe, Africa and Asia. No one suspected that the world had another world. A vast new world. The solitute of Latin America. The land of chronicles, with fantastic stories handed down from generation to generation, as Garcia Marquez says (1983), "that-immense fatherland of dazzled men and historical women, whose obstinancy is confounded with legend.

America did not have a name. It was anonymous, like the serpents and the curiously carved logs coming far from the Atlantic... The Norwegians did not know they had discovered it long ago. Admiral Columbus himself died convinced he had reached Asia by the western route to India. When the conquistador boats and swords first trod the sands of the Bahamas, Columbus thought that these islands were an outpost of the fabulous Isle of Zipango, Japan. He was mistaken. It was America.

America, America... Yes! They have hurt us. And we cannot forget those wounds. They also confirm our experience. A part of our personality is at risk of becoming lost between the wastes of violence... Perhaps we cannot see now, that from its ruins will emerge a new man and a permanent peace.

3

Perhaps. Facing history. For what purpose history? Searching? It could not be a mere collection of dates, an accumulation of wars and loss, losing from remote times. Most contemporary analysis will avoid the focus of these facts with resentement. Yes! It is very valid to search in the past, above all is our history. It is Latin American history. It is our daily violence. It is our hopeless peace. Yes, it is valid to search in our past. It is valid for locating our present situation. It is valid whether we look with a critical mind at the past, sincere thoughts. The judgement of past is made of our own sensations of our own problems, and of our own limitations. However, this is not a journey into the past. It is an attempt to actualize our past. The wealth of legends does not make us less historical. On the contrary, it makes us break the tender balance between truth and fantasy, between research and creation. Indeed, it is a question to the past, whose answer is reflected in the reality of a continuous present.

This essay expresses a critical view of Latin American history, whose main characteristic is violence: a continuous aggression in opposition to its life and cultural forms. The appearance of the concept of dependency as a basic factor of analysis has been of relevant importance in the explanation of the historical and social processes of Latin America. But .it is necessary to focus the dependency as a structural condition of the societies, which irnplies at the same time the study of such

4

process -of the dependent societies-, as part of a world historical process. This perspective conducts to integrate as an unique system the problem of modern industrial countries and its results in the underdeveloped countries. One and other play a specific role in the developrnent of the whole system. In this paper concerning Latin Amamrican peace, dependency will appear as a true element of each national society, and the study of violence -aggression or instability- could not be realized without reference to the whole global system (Vasconi, 1969; and Quijano, 1971).

The theory of dependency, or dependencia, is the expression of a Latin American analysis about its particular historical and social antecedents. Since the Second World War, Latin American scholars have come to see themselves as underdeveloped, in the concept of ideological and econornic irnplications. During the 1950s at the Econornic Commission for Latin America -ECLA-, this concept was the central theme of concern. To some extend it was the response to the neo-classical theory of monetarism adopted by most of the Latin American countries. The fact that the policy of import substitution created new forms of dependency converted this concept into theory. Then, it was considered that the world consisted of a "core" of dominant nations and a "periphery"of dependent ones. Its main feature is, however, an emphasis on external influences that distort the process of development, whose influence leads to an historical approach. Another characteristic is that the theory stresses political and cultural influences as well as economic ones.

Indeed, some echoes of the dependency theory reach Europe as well, because some structural rigidities of European countries are conspicuous too, especially in areas geographically on the periphery, such as Turkey, Greece, Italy, Spain, Portugal, Ireland and Britain, amongst others. Perhaps such rigidities are not quite so dramatically visible as in Latin America, but most of them are increasingly dependent on the core of Europe, and all, including the most advanced, have been deeply penetrated by foreign based transnational corporations. Hence, the relevance of the theory as a methodology for the study of concrete situations of dependency. For this, we can conclude that its principal contribution is the attempt to analyse peripheral societies through a comprehensive social science, which stresses the socio-political and historical nature of Latin American development (Seers, 1983).

Our starting point is that any interpretation of peace in Latin America requires the concept of dependency for its explanation. Thus, three different cases of an historical approach will produce three different forms of extreme: (1) The first of Spanish origin, resulted in a brutal exploitation during the colonial period, whose most clear example was the sugar culture -so called the "white gold"- of the tropical coasts and Caribbean islands, (2) The second stage a feature of the liberal economic system during the XIXth century and beginning of the last century led to a series of military aggressions and dictatorships whose major examples were the so called "banana republics" of Central America, and (3) finally, the industrial neo-colonial dependency, which has resulted in a deep cultural transformation of the Latin American societies. The most prominent case is that of the oil extraction -"black-gold"- in Venezuela. These ideas are complemented by this introduction, followed by a second chapter which is related to the way of living of our indigenous ancestors before the discovery of America, then a chapoter where the three cases are presented, and a final chapter is concerned with the present situation -of terror and human rights violations- of a modern continent which profoundly contrasts with the ancient perspective.

We have something to say to the forgotten Mayan god Huitzilopochtli. We have something to add to the murder of Atahualpa, the Inca. We must say something. When the conquistador boats first trod the warm sands...

CHAPTER I. THE ANCIENT TIME

One of the cardinal preoccupation of man in all epoch has been to search and find his origins. This, sometimes becomes a fundamental problem for his future, and a necessity of his daily life. All this, because the mystery of his origin is a sentiment born with the first flashes of his reflective intellectuality. That instant, is when the idea is conscious and becomes life. To exist is being, it is to reflect. Indeed, it is to live. The concern of many written works and scholars of this slow ascent of the human being and his mind show to what extent this study reaffirms the evidence of the relationship between space and time in man. The past, seen in this way – whether under a materialist dialectic view or through mitic-religious metaphisics- has meaning only if future man is located in his present day in his far past.

It is difficul t to image how the indigenous American realized his own reality, his mythology. The research of philosophers and scientits in the antiquity gave an ethnocentric view of the Americans. It is at least a perception of his reality, a mixture of legends and fables. It was the pre-scientific opinion of Baudeau, Las Casas, Buffon, and de Pawn. But after a short time, man bacame mankind and in turn, the Americans. These savage people knew stone weapons and that was the clue to establish a link with their prehistoric utensils. Then, it had a presentiment of a vague notion of evolutionism. The European Renaissance changed this ethnocentric view, setting a hierarchy of human values which converted inevitability to racism. The monsters changed their image!

The Americans -Andeans, Mesoamericans or Amazons- created their original world on the basis of a severe organization of the economy, and a hieratic perspective of the society as a whole, model impregnated by a strong religious belief. This model produces its own weakness: they did not achieve any unity. This young empire, initiated a regressive cosmic cycle, through the path of mitic fatalism, accepting its own uprooting. TheAmericans were abandoned by their gods. The cities were divided. Then began the political conflicts. Finally, the Indian army was overthrown. A unique idiom, a unique God, and a unique King substituted the tradition of millennias. The American world cannot escape from its ruin, and. every day is distanced from its own history without possibl1ity of re-encountering it.

The Mesoamericans and the Andeans have been called Testimonny Peoples for they are the survivors of the old civilizations defeated by the impact of European expansionism. Tropical countries in turn, were called New Peoples. Thus they entered into an acculturation process which has continued until the present day. The Spaniards found in these regions huge cities with a cultural tradition completely different from their own. After the Spanish invasion, both the Mesoamerican - Mexicans and Mayas of Central America-, and the Andean societies collapsed.

Although today, all these peoples are independent nations, never have they been as they were, rather victims of the violent transformation imposed upon them, the adaptation to new conditions of economic systems, and the impact of the Mercantile and Industrial Revolutions. More than peoples deferred in their history, they are despoiled by their own history (Ribeiro, 1969).

There, they are, Teotihuacan, Chan-chan, Chichen Itza, resembling our past. We just can remember the sad glories of Chilem Balam and the endless route to the Sun, present still. After lamentable omens, appeared Quetzacoalt, then Uiracocha and Kon Tiki. The Americans remain placed in the violence which is extended to all spirits: the Guadalupe Virgin became God Tonantzin, too. The Inca Garcilaso become our first exiled. At the same time, the cities grew in the continent and with them temples, pyramids and streets: Yucatán, Palenque, Uxmal, Labna, Zayi. In all the Mesoamerican peoples, even now, the indigenous dimension persisits in a relevant form. And indeed it was one of the thighest expressions of human artistry.

In the centre and southern areas of todays Mexico flourished the Aztec culture, and in Guatemala the Maya, both achieved an urban era with a wide commercial system, a deeply stratified society, and a complex political structure, similar to the states, but more vast. Mexico was inhabited by the Aztecs of Nahualt idiom, whose federative organization included three centres, Texcoco, Tlacopan, and Tenochtitlán. They had their own writing system, a precise calendar, and an urban development which was comparable with the Egyptian or Babilonic. The Mayas were considered one of the biggest and original cultures of the world, though lower than the Egyptian. They were an agricultural people, with writing and mathematical systems, and with outstanding sculptures. What is important about the Mayas is that they were probably the first civilization which flourished in a tropical rain forest, creating a model of urban structure especially adapted to these ecological conditions, a preamble of the future tropical cities.

On the contrary, in the Andeans, the culture was opposed to the Aztecs and Mayas in that it was less mystic, and with a more profound organization which permitted them to assemble strong theocratic empire. For this, their transport system was well established linking Cuzco, the capital, with the rest of the altiplane territory. This enabled them to communicate with all the small towns and about 10 million of their inhabitants. They had to adapt an inhospitable region with high mountains and with land of little use for agricultural purposes. But they became masters in the use of ploughed terraces.

All these cultures grew without mutual influence, for they were develpped in a independent way. Their cardinal features were the collective social organization, the theocratic state -centralized- and a well establish agricultural system. The number of inhabitants in that America is not clear yet. Some authors state a figure of between 6-9 million (Kroeber, 1939; Steward, 1949; Rosenblat, 1954). Recent studies indicate an amount of about 30 million for Central Mexico (Borach and Cook, 1963). Other writers suggest about 13 million for Central America and about 37 million for the Andeans (Dobyns and Thompson, 1966). According to these last studies, it is possible to assume that these empires, as a whole, had between 70-80 mlllion of inhabitants before the conquest. A century and half later, and due to the violent impact of this process, those settlementshad been reduced to 3.5 million. This was the means by which Europeanand the American cultures entered in colonial conjuction. Sad destiny. A handful of two hundred thousand Spanish dominated millions of indigenous people, melting them into a different cultural complex, whose base was the Iberic root.

Today Latin Americans are the result of more than two hundred years of latinity and the mixture of European, African, and Indian peoples. They are the inheritors of a multiple culture fused under compulsory slavevery of the Spanish expansion. In other words, they are a civilization as old as the most ancient in culture, and at the same time as new as the newest peoples. The old inheritance reflects their worse characteristics such as social discrimination between rich and poor, the conformism, and resignation of the poor with their poverty. The new is manifest in the vigorous assertion of the poor that misery and violence are not inevitable, in their pride to be an ethnic mixture, half-breed, and in their consequent rebellion against the status-quo, trying to bring a new epoch of progrese and peace. An ancient poem of the half-gods of the Quiche Hunahpuand Ixbalanché peoples, against the genius of evil -owners of the dark kingdom of Xibalba- seems once again relevant:

> Oíd nuestros nombres. Os diremos también los nombres de nuestros padres. Nosotros somos Ixhunalpú e Ixbalanqué, estos son nuestros nombres. Y nuestros padres son aquellos que matásteis y que se llaman Hun-Hunahpu y Vuoub-Hunahpu. Nosotros los que aquí véis, somos, pues, los vengadores de los dolores y sufrimientos de nuestros padres. Por eso nosotros sufrimos todos los males que les hicísteis. En consecuencia os acabaremos a todos vosotros, os daremos muerte y ninguno escapará, les dijeron. (Popol Vuh, 1973, p.19)

> (Listen to our names. We will tell you also the name of our parents. We are Ixhunalpú and Ixbalanqué, these are our names. Our parents are those whom you

14

murdered, named Hun-Hunahpu, and Vuoub-Hunahpu We are then, as you can see, the avengers of the pains and sufferings of our parents. For this, we are suffering all the evils you did. Therefore, we will exterminate you all. We will kill you and none one will escape, they said). (Trans. L. Chesney).

CHAPTER II. THE DEPENDENCY

PROCESS: THREE CASES

1492 was the year of the discovery of America. It was also the time of a deep crisis in the western world, which extended to the economic, scial and sritual area The political scenario followed a similar trend. The theory of a morality with double face prevailed and the works of Machiaveli were famous (Hauser, 1976). These were the predominant ideas which influenced the conquerors of the New World, and oriented their relationship with the India, as Admiral Columbus called then America.

For martial Spain, 1492 was also the year of the recovery of Granada, the storming of the last Arab positions on Sapnish soil. It had. taken nearly eight centuries to win what was lost in seven years (Elliot, 1965). That same year, 150.000 Jews were expelled from the Peninsula. Spain went forward wielding swords with the Sign of the Cross on their hilts. This military heritage, coming from the tradition of the medieval crusading wars, and religious enthusiasm, provided a halo for the conquest of new lands beyond the ocean.

Three years after the discovery of America, Columbus personally directed the military campaign against the indigenous indians of Dominicana. When he first landed on San Salvador atoll, he realized they knew nothing of swords, and "when these were shown to them they grasped the sharp edges and cut themselves" (Galeano, p.20). On his third voyage, the Admiral still believed he was in the China Sea, when he was nearly off the aoast of Venezuela. Thus, the epic of the Spaniards and Portuguese in America, combined propagation of the Christian faith with extermination and plunder of native wealth.

The discovery went on. The Treaty of Tordesillas (1494), allowed Portugal to occupy American territories: in 1530, Martin Alfonso de Sousa founded the first Portuguese cities in Brazil. Meanwhile, the Spaniards had advanced far in the conquest. In 1513, Vasco Nuñez de Balboa explored the South Pacific.In 1522, Ferdinand Magallan's returned, he who had for the first time united both oceans and confirmed that the world was round. In 1519, Hernán Cortes sailed from Cuba towards México. In 1523, Pedpo de Alvarado launched the conquest of Central America. In 1533, Francisco Pizarro entered Cuzco, the heart of the Inca Empire, and in 1540, Pedro de Valdivia founded Santiago de Chile.

So, Spanish expansion started from the European concept of the city. Many cities were established throughout the region, substituting the indigenous villages which had been constructed before the XVIth century. These new cities signalled the initial step of a deep process of "transculturation" by means of which the Americans lost their freedom to accept or refuse imposed cultural and social patterns (Ortíz, 1976). To achieve this end were used two mechanisms:(1) the physical extermination of indigenous leaders, and (2) by diminishing the population through intense conditions of work, epidemic transmission, and ecological disturbance. The indigenous way of life witnessed its own disintegration and the emergence of a direct dependence to the metropolis.

The term transculturation (transculturación, in spanísh), is a Latin American neologism created in 1929 by Dr. Fernando Ortíz, Cuban anthropologist (1881-1969). Accoraing to Bronislaw Malinowsky, in his introduction to the book *Contrapunto cubano*, by Ortiz, transculturation is the new technical word to substitute several expressions in use such as "culture change",. "acculturation", "diffusion", and others which Ortíz considered to be unsuitable. Therefore, transculturation may be seen as an interchange of cultures and civilizations.

The "white gold"of the tropical coasts and Caribbean islands

Although the aims of the Conquest were gold and silver, Columbus on his second voyage brought the first sugarcane roots from the Canary Islands and planted them in what is now the Dominican Republic. Sugar was a precious article to the Europeans. Thus, was the most important item for European commerce. Canefields grew in the tropical littoral of Northeast Brazil and in the Caribbean Islands -Barbados, Jamaica, Haiti, St. Domingo, Guadalupe, Cuba, and Puerto Rico, in Veracruz and the Peruvian coast which became the best lands for the "white gold". Legions of slaves came from Africa to provide the labour force required, "human fuel" for the burning. The long sugar cycle generated an artificial prosperity. Curiously, three distinct historical periods -mercantilism, feudalism, and slavery- were combined in each canefield. These colonial plantations evolved directly into the present "latifundio", they being a continuing problem which prevent rural development and condemn the peasantry to poverty and a margiñal existence in Latin America. After the peak of the sugar cycle, and due to competition from substitute products, exhaustion of the soils, and the development of new economic areas, came decay. The Northeast was Brazil's richest region, now it is the poorest. The same effect occurred in the Caribbean "sugar-islands". Because of the sugar cycle, Haiti became converted into a slavery dump. By 1786-1787, the French colony had brought in sixty-seven thousand slaves. But revolution broke out in 1791. By 1802, the once flourishing colony was in ashes and ruins, half of the black people exterminated and a order of that not a single mulatto with epaulets must be left in the colony. Haiti was born poor, was devastated, and never recovered, until now.

Such exploltation of both natural and human resources has been seen to take the same role for cocoa in Caracas, for cotton in Maranhao, for rubbar in the Amazon territory, for the devastated "quebracho"-forests in Northern Argentina and Paraguay, for henequen plantations in Yucatán, for coffe in Central America, for the fruit plantations in Brazil, Colombia and Central American countries.

The liberal economic system during the XIX-XXth centuries

The Independence period taken by Latin American countries at the end of XVIIIth century, orientated a change in the dependency process. Independence, as a revolutionary myth, was only an expression at the super-structural level of society and became inevitably a transformation of the old system from mercantilism to the industrial stage. Consequently, this changed the "core" of the dependency. The ideological framework of this transference was the Laissez-faire theory, physiocracy, and the Manchesterian economic system. Its aim was the conquest of markets (Vasconi, 1969).

At the end of the last century, Central America was transformed. By 1880 its recently built coffee plantations produced only for the international market; But early this century "banana stands" made their appearance in Honduras, Guatemala, Costa Rica and Colombia.

The first banana cultivators of the Bahia Islands, never realized the importance this product would acquired in the history of Central America in future decades. Those buds originally established as decorative gardens, became by 1899 the extensive plantations of the United Fruit Company -the famous "chiquita

21

banana"- of Honduras, and then across all Central America. In 1929, the depression caused a drop in the price of bananas, the investment stopped and consequently unemployment and the displacement of peasants occurred. The people reacted with strikes. Social agitation was repressed violently through the already implanted dictatorships. They were to remain in power for the following twenty years: Jorge Ubico of Guatemala, Maximiliano Hernandez of El Salvador, Tiburcio Carias of Honduras, and Anastacio Somoza of Nicaragua. The long struggle of Augusto Cesar Sandino ended in 1979, when the dictator Somoza Jr. fled from the country. Forty-five years have passed since the murder of General Sandino, who once said "my army and I, are the natural consequence of the criminal and absurd foreign policy of Northamerica in Nicaragua". During 1982, came the first free-elections of El Salvador, after fifty years of military governments and sucessive coup d'etats. The resulting confrontation, during the period of 1979-1981, produced over 30,000 persons dead and of more than 450,000 refugees in neighbourign countries, without international status or aid.

Dramatic and difficult is the history of Central America, especially in its relationship with the United States. It could not be different when the latter considers the region, including the Caribbean nations, for its geopolitical expansion. This may be seen as the reason why the United States has never permitted a united region, rather seeking to divide its nations into weak republics and maintain them with an uncertain future. On the other hand, the Central American republics, underdeveloped and poor, are the most elocuent example of an imposed model of development, whose main feature is an economic and political submission. These "banana-republics" are an example to the world of what this type of model has to offer. Indeed, it is amazing to think that these countries were once the ancient and great Mesoamerican civilizations.

The geopolitical aims of the United States place Central America as a centre for its expansionist policy. All presidents have followed the dictates of this "Manifest Destiny". At least 784 hostile actions have been undertaken against the sovereignty of the Latin America-and Caribbean countries. Since 1960, more than 100 have occurred in Central American countries. The itinerary of this journey is extensive. President Jefferson (1801-1809), who inspined the Monroe Doctrine, expressed his fear that Spain could not resist the independence struggle of the Latin American countries until the United States was strong enough to be in a position of gradually absorbing these colonies under its own sphere of influence (Kharchatourov, 1977).

When the Monroe Doctrine was promulgated, it was not seen as a threat by the Latin Americans, for they were still struggling for their independence of Spain. However, Simón Bolívar –Liberator of Venezuela, Colombia, Ecuador, Perú, and Bolivia– gave a strong warning of this future prospect (Pividal, 1970, p. 171).

During the middle of the XIXth century, W. Walker invaded Central America and proclaimed himself President of Nicaragua, El Salvador, and Honduras, where he restored slavery. By 1912, President W. Taft expressed "the whole hemisphere will be ours in fact as, by virtue of our superiori ty of race, it already is ours morally" (Selser, 1962). During the same period, ex-president Theodore Roosevelt determined the establishment of the Republic of Panamá, dividing the Colombian territory and recalling "I took the Canal Zone and let Congress debate". Later on, he will be winner of the Nobel Peace Prize.

Only after the United States-Spain war of 1898 -when Cuba was liberated and Puerto Rico annexed- did Washington assume the right of "tutor" of the destiny of the Caribbean. President Roosevelt exposed the hidden philosophy behind their policy of the "big-stick": The United States would become an international police force in order to maintain order and peace in the continent. Through this doctrine the United States claimed the right to intervene in Latin America and the Caribbean.

In 1927, Calvin Coolidge sent Marines back to Nicaragua, in order to "save" it from "bolshevism" imported from the Mexican revolution, then considered as the communist bogeyman of Latin America. When they withdrew, eight years later, The United States rewarded the Nicaraguans with the dynaatic Somoza dictatorship, which for the next 43 years tyrannized the people. In 1932, when Franklin D. Roosevelt assumed the presidency, came the era of "the good neighbour policy". This resulted in the murder of Sandino and a complete network of dictatorships to replace the resident Marines. This was the bananization of Central

America. In 1954, Jacobo Arbenz, President of Guatemala was overthrown, accused of being a "communist". Dwight D. Eisenhower -authorized the Central Intelligence Agency to "destabilize" the legitimately elected government. This occurred because Arbenz had accepted political support from a local communist party, and had attempt to expropiate some of the United Fruit properties. Then followed a succession of brutal rightist military regimes.

In 1961, John F. Kennedy reaffirmed this path by launching The Bay of Pigs invasion. Its failure, strengthened the Cuban revolution and left The United States frustrated and angry. As a consequence of this, President Kennedy promoted "The Alliance for Progress", which provided urgent economic aid to some Latin American countries. This was done in order to avoid another Cuba coming into existence. However, despite this policy in 1965, Lyndon B. Johnson sent 400 Marines into the Dominicári Republic to rescue 18 "Americans in danger". This invasion force was increased to 20,000 men when a few "known comunists" were discovered in the country.

In 1973, the Nixon Admiistration undertook to "destabilize" the elected Chilean government of President Salvador Allende.

Chile was rewarded with General Pinohet, one of the bloodier tyrants in modern Latin America history. In 1981, President Reagan promoted a new policy of "true friendship and brotherhood" in order to assure the stability of the zone. This idea was concreted in the Symms Amendment which authorized the President to impede any Cuban aggression, using all means, including weapons. This Amendment was modified by Congress and transformed into Bumpers Amendment, which indicates that this law does not authorized the President to overlook the Security Act of 1947 and a Resolution on the war attributions of 1973.

Then came Grenada, the small victory that the United States needed to cure themselves of the remaining fears left over after its defeat in Vietnam. George W. Ball (1983) stated that the United states will intervene "in what is historically considered our sphere". This statement is intended to legitimate interventions in Latin America, when it is suspected that a capitalist country is being threatened with a revolution, socialist regime, or any progressive change. Nevertheless, The United states may be seen to be engaged in a dangerous policy of external interventions against peoples ready to give their lives before giving up their struggle for freedom and the right of autodetermination.

The case of the oil extraction
-the "black-gold"-

The last five decades have made more clear the appearence of this new "core" of dependency, and this fact is closely connected with the establishment of an international network of monopolies, which have evolved throughout the Continente At the same time, this has been the period in which a breaking with our indigenous heritage is clearly visible. The watchword at present expresses the necessity to re-examine all things.

During the seventies and eighties, the majority of the Latin American political systems were under the complete control of the national armies. Only a few four or five nations can be given the wide qualification of being called democratic. As ever, these military dictatorships were in power with the aim of acting as guarantors for the-future of their countries, insisting upon the necessity of an undefined period of time to restate the values and relations of power.

The outcome has resulted in a lack of confidence in democracy. Far from a positive end, the search for new options continues. Curiously -and this can be seen as an example of the effect of a neocolonialist industrial dependency- the Latin American country most historically identified with militarism, "caudillismo", and dictatorship -Venezuela-, at that time and up until 1990, was the most persistent democracy of the Continente. The Venezuelan leadership seemed to have learned the lesson that a military ideology, at the end, has to give away to the re-enstatement of the cardinal values of democracy. From 1958, the Venezuelan democracy had persisted although the power is alternated between two traditional parties. Technically, it seemed that democracy in Venezuela has instituted. Nevertheless, this triumph rested on the angular stone of its national development: oil rent. No other factor explained better the Venezuelan democracy, in profound contrast with the wild view of militarism in Latin America duriong the seventies.

Oil was not unknow inVenezuela. During the colonial period it was used only for -domesticpurposes -the "mene" was the name given by the indigenous people to oil-. By 1882 the Petrolia of Tachira Company existed, exploiting the so called asphalt-oil. Venezuela lacked the proper-technology and between 1913 to 1917 the drilling was undertaken by British, Dutch and Northamerican companies. By 1922, the éxplosíon of Barroso well in Zulia state, revealed inmense reserves of oil in the region, and therefore the investment increased. The revenues of currency and the commerce resulting from the oil industry transformed Venezuela abruptly from an agrarian country into a modernization era, an ideal market for imports and consumption.

The change has been profound and rapid. The dependencyon oil has increased. The first effect of this impact was the spacial displacementof the Venezuelans with all its implications. By 1936, 34.7% of the population lived in urban zones. By 1980, already 80% lived in cities. During the same period the population increased four times. The riches of oil, have enabled the State to promote notable development in the metalurgic and hydroelectric sectors of the economy, but the system as a whole had not an independent life. Everything has a connection with this derived rent. So, oil did not altered the permanent condition of economic dependency, as always Venezuelan society has submitted to mono-cultures and the decisions of transnational enterprises.

In the past, it was the same with the pearls and gold, then the cocoa, and now oil. In contrast, thanks to oil and its artificial riches, a democratic system can be guaranteed –an unusual example to Latin America- resulting in the emergence of a powerful middle-class, non existent 50 years ago.

Perhaps the most disruptive impact has been the transculturation produced by oil. It has profoundly changed the way of living and being of the Venezuelans. The roots of this culture change came from the establishement of the oil indastry and with the consequential international pressures placed upon the country (i.e. mass-media technology). The national identity of the Venezuelans is not precise and profound. A nationalist reaction put on the table this question of identity. The transculturative process, from the conquest to the present has been violent, traumatic and brief. The diversity of elements are not yet composed. This explains the mixture of our population with indians, peasants, urban marginals, and modern elites. Only the indigenous people are excluded from this process. The rest are deeply affected in their comportment, values and .even through language, by the mass-media, by the import of consumer goods, and by a saturation of commercial publicity. All this is sustained economically by the rent oif the oil boom. Venezuelan society has passed from a slow traditional style to an extremely accelerated modern one without assuming its culture.

The result has been over consumption, social uprooting, and an ecological damage in nature. The country seems not to have a dimension of time:"our cities could be erected in Texas or Kuwait, because all in them is new, without modules nor proper character of any order"(Liscano, 1980). In 1974, the oil industry was nationalized, but it did not break its links with the international companies in aspects of refining and marketing. The pace of society has changed: "all seem to be late in Venezuela". Indeed, when we record its reality, this has already changed. Venezuela is a Tropical, Andean, Caribbean, Atlantic, and Amazonic country with a vast horizon. Unfortunately, its future is strictly determined.through a programme controlled by powerful international interests. May be, for this reason the life there is sudden.

Where the country is going now since the begining of the XXIth century? Nowhere. We were a rural society, illiterate, unhealthy, unable to exercise democracy. But in the span of a decade, from the late twenties of the XXth century, unexpectedly began to change and the country began to be up-date, growing, and so became one of the most prosperous economy not only of Latin America but also in the world. That was the miracle that produced oil! From then until the eighties of the last century, while the world quintupled its living standards, and Latin America tripled, Venezuela increased tenfold! Six decades of grow, rapidly and without problems. Six decades of peace and stability. But then, suddendly it started to decrease, and broke the thread of the story: we entered into a general crisis. It was a strange road, again sad and difficult, still are producing oil.

Now, as 100 years ago, when the country again stands still, we turn to ask what horizon do we have? The answer is the same as yesterday: oil. But there is a difference with what happened a century ago, now the Venezuelan State is the sole owner of oil, is rich, the country is a modern one, but corrupt, and the people are poor. The State became the richest trader in the country, the opposite of before. Therefore, from the 1980s, there is a generation of youngVenezuelans who have not known the development, but only the crisis.

The collapse of the Venezuelan society living on oil rent brought an overwhelming political storm that has brought back the country to the past, in a fruitless search for lost time. Already too late to return to that idyllic past rentierism. Now, they face a new and dramatic reality of this country: the economic and political power is in one hand, the hand of an inefficient ruler, with vast oil revenues which are wasted while poverty is growing by leaps and bounds. Look at some numbers, more than 60% of the country is now poor, high unemployment, strong devaluation of its currency, increasing inflation, low human development, increases malnutrition and tropical diseases or pests, low milk consumption for children, corruption increases. But there is something more serious that accompanies all this, in recent years, a Court in London and other in Canada have certified that Venezuela violate human rights and that torture is used by the security organs of the military government. In addition to this, the regime showed no mercy against the oil workers, when more than 22 thousand oil technicians of high level were fired from their jobs, and their families were subject to harassment, eviction from their homes occupied and their children were denied enrollment in their schools. This is the paradox of the oil boom. Now the country face an authoritarian regime. Some day, someone might ask why the Venezuelans plenty of oil arriveds to this sad destiny?

CHAPTER III. THE PRESENT TIME

The term Latin America is closely connected with the ideas of Simón Bolívar -The Liberator-. It comes from his notion of a "grand homeland" fused in the creation of the Great-Colombia, and extended by José Martí with his dream of "Our America". But the concept of Latin America, based on these premises, has only been used during our century and particularly at the present time. Todays re-emergence of the ideas of "The Liberator" can be seen to receive careful attention from the two hegemonic powers of the world. Thus, the international conflicts of the individual Latin American countries are not envisaged as small and provincial areas of focus, but global political problems.

This is the present reality, whether we like it or noto It is a complex reality with a strong component of inter-relationships. But this concept oí Latin American today, does not mean a complete unity. What is remarkable is a fundamental conciousness of continental cohesion, especially amongst the people. We must remember that our main historical sickness has been "non-unity". Our experience has shown that unity is only achieved when external threat comes.

The past seems to be ever present in todays Latin America. Externally imposed conflicts seem to be the price of this relative unity of the people. Conflicts still exist in Central America, an yet not militar interventions. Past history is again reflected in present day events. Once more, Central America has become a focus of attention in the world. The only valid explanation to this situation is found in the analysis of the historical factors of the zone. Continuing instability, varying between revolution and dictatorship, has been-the destiny of our continent.

The most dramatic example of fascism in Latin America was found in Chile. The socialist transition project of President Salvador Allende, affecting foreign interests as it did opened an external front which finally was perverseness and inexorable, resulting in military intervention. This was a serious mistake. Since the ninety, and after the fall of the Berlin wall, democracy has returned. The Chilean people, once the self-considered Britons of South America, now share the same history as the rest of the countries of the region. They have paid a high price to discover that they could not go on living from myths and fables.

The same phenomenon was repeated in Argentina. The army was not prepared for either governing nor struggling. The country was deeply shaken by the defeat of the Malvinas - Falklands- Islands war, and consequently re-encountered its unity in a new democracy and in a continental solidarity to its cause. Argentina, the most European country of the continent, now knows it is Latin American as well.

After more than ten years, the Uruguayan dictatorship remained isolated from the rest of the Latin American countries, The Uruguayan people, once self-considered the Swiss of South America, now are united and living in democracy, receiving absolute solidarity from the dernocratic countries of the region.

After a terrible decade of the eigthies, sorne countries in Latin America arrived at a peaceful rest along a rough road. The transit from military dictatorship or authoritarian rulers -modern versions of fascism- to democracy has been hard, but it is possible, thanks to the unity of the people. Another process of a dernocratic aperture, although slower, was Brazil where the pressure of the people has obligated the Generals to call for democracy. Peru also has returned to a democratic system after trying all kinds of military government, rightist and nationalist. In other countries, democracy still falters as in the case of Venezuela, Bolivia, and Ecuador, with authoritarian regimes since the ninety.

It is interesting to observe the efforts made by the Catholic Church in order to bring evidence of the violation of human rights and to support social justice in Central America and in the rest oif the Continent. The Church, guided by the Puebla Conference's theme of "a preferential option for the poor and by a commitment to defend human rights" has been described by many countries as a "subversive force". The Church also has emphasized the historical perspective of the conflict through The United States Bishops' Testimony to Congress (1983), stating that the position of the

Church is clearly defined and its role in the region hardly can be confused with Marxist interests. On the contrary, its pastoral aim is guided by a teaching based on the Gospels but profoundly committed to the defence of human rights.

Carlos Fuentes (1983), the Mexican writer, represents the general Latin American opinion when he clearly identifies the main conflicts in the region and their alternative solutions:"The problems of Cuba are Cuban... The problems of Nicaragua are Nicaraguan ... many of our countries are struggling to cease being banana republics. They do not want to become balalaika republics. Do not force them to choose..."

Latin America appears in our search througs history as an unique camp, complex and variable. Perhaps non-existent in itself. Reality shows that few Latin American peoples live as individual nations. It is indeed as Sartre said "a being that is what is not, and it is not what it is". For us, that which has been imposed over five centuries is our differentiation. The different heritage of the conqueror in Perú, the Caribbean, New Spain, La Plata, the original zones of the present nations. But, for the image of "the other", from the beginning we were a unique world. The novelty of The New World eliminated its own diversity. Thus, for the Europeans we were always a whole -as John Donne would say, "that unripe side of earth"- where industrial countries meet their necesities of cheap materials, a source of additional markets for their products, a place for foreign investment of capital, and recently an area for operation of the multinationals (Cohen, 1974). Our challenge is to give an accurate out-line of Latin America, which we believe is not only possible, but necessary for our future. For this we reject that view coming from "the other", for it follows the maintenance of our Continent in the present situation, divided, uprooted, and alienated after more than five centuries of dependency.

Obviously, any improvement in our situation has to be made on the basis of questioning our dependency through the elimination of our compliance to external pressures and all things leading to dependence and its hidden unit total extermination. In contrast, we must assume an attitude of liberation and autodetermination. The problem is to pass from the first to the second one, after such long period of docility. The first coul be a approach is to concentrate on i ts effects on our area. This is a compulsory task. This is not defeatism nor reactionism, especially if we take into account the displacement of the global powers from the socio-economic sphere to the ideological and military one, which implies the highest degree of rational violence (Abdel-Malek, 1977). The socialist sentiment can aid our reconstruction, but the phenomenon itself remains unchangeable: the world enters an epoch of universal dependency. For a majority of the Latin Americans, the only way possible is a deep sociopolitical change. Either through a democracy or revolutionary process, the internal relationships must change.

"This is my friends, the knot of our solitute", said Gabriel García Marquez (1983), winner of the Nobel Literature Prize. He added, "perhaps the venerable Europa would be most comprehensive if it tried to see us in its own past. If it recalled that London needed 300 years to construct its first wall and other 300 to appoint a bishop... But I think Europeans of clear spirit, those who also fought here for a grand and more just fatherland, could help us better if they reviewed in a profound sense the way they see us... his is my friends, the size of our solitude". After studying our reality, we find out on the one hand the spuriousness of our history and on the other hand the possibility of Latin America.

Latin America will change. We will overcome dependency. We will enter into the dialogue of the whole world, for we have a specific contribution to civilization. This contribution will consist, fundamentally in expressing as Ribeiro (1969) stated, what we are as a social, historical and cultural configuration: more human, for we will incorporate all cultural features of man. More generous, for we remain open to all influences and we will integrate all race. More progressive, for our future is founded only in the development of knowledge. More optimism, for we will emerge from the exploitation and poverty, and we know that the future will be better than the past and the present. And also more free, for our national projects will be undertaken not assuming oppression nor spoliation of other peoples.That would be our peace.

Soton (U.K)- Caracas (Ven)/ 84-11.

REFERENCES

Abdel-Malek, A. (1977). *Sociología del Imperialismo*. México. U.N.A.M.

Ball,W.G. (1983). "America's version of the Brezhnew Doctrine". The Guardian (International ed.). 26 June, p. 8.

Borach,W. and Cook, S. F. (1963). *The Aboriginal Population of Central Mexico on the Eve of the Spanish Conquest*. Berkeley.

Bras, J. M. (1983). "Puerto Rico:Agenda Inconclusa de Bolívar". El Nacional (Caracas), 8.July, p. A-8.

Cohen, B.J. (1974). *The question of Imperialism:The Political Economy of Dominance and Dependence*. London. Macmillan.

Dobyns,H. and Thompson, P. (1966). "Estimating Aboriginal American Population". *Current Anthropology* 7-4. Utrecht. Netherlands.

Dudley,S. (Ed.) (1983).*Dependency Theory. A Critical Reassessment*. Reprint, London. Frances Pinter Publ.

Elliot, J.H. (1963). *Imperial Spain*. London.

Fuentes, Carlos (1983)."Do not Force us to Become your Enemy". The Guardian (International Ed.), June, 21.

Galeano, Eduardo (1979). *Las Venas Abiertas de America Latina*. México. Siglo XXI. 26 Ed. enlarged, trans. by C. Belfrage in 1 Ed.

Holland, S. and Anderson, D. (1984). *Kissinger's Kingdom?* (A Counter-Report on Central America). Preface by Neil Kinnock MP. Nottingham. Russel Press Ltd.

Hauser, A. (1976). *The Social History of Art*. Madrid. Guadarrama. Vol. I. Trans. by A. Tovar and F.P. Varas.

Khatchatourov, K. (1977). "The Writings of Thomas Jefferson-1858". Le Monde Diplomatic. February, p.11.

Kroeber, A. L. (1939). *Cultural and Natural Areas of Native North America.* Berkeley. Univ. California.

Liscano, Juan (1980). ¿Identidad Nacional o Universalidad? Caracas. Ed. El Diario de Caracas. Col Libros de Hoy. No.57, pp.16-17.

Márquez, Gabriel García (1983). "La Soledad de América Latina". *Rev. KoEyu Latinoamericano.* No. 28, pp. 30-32 (trans. by L. Chesney).

Ortíz, Fernando (1976). *Contrapunteo Cubano del Tabaco y del Azúcar.* Caracas. Biblioteca Ayacucho No.42.

Pividal, P. F. (1977). *Bolívar: Pensamiento Precursor del Antiimperialismo.* La Habana. Casa de las Américas, p.171.

Popol Vuh (1973). *Las Antiguas Historias del Quiché.* México. E.F.C.E.

Quijano, A. (1971). "Cultura y Dominación". *Rev. Latinoamericana de Ciencias Sociales.* Jun-Dic.

Ribeiro, Darcy (1969). *Las Américas y la Civilización.* Buenos Aires. Centro Ed. de America Latina. Vol. I.

Rosenblat, A. (1954). *La Población Indígena y el Mestizaje en América Latina.* Buenos Aires. 2 Vol.

Seers, D (Ed.) (1983). *Dependency Theory: A Critical Reassessment.* Reprint. London. Frances Pinter Pub.

Selser, G. (1962). *Diplomacia, Garrote y Dólares en América Latina.* Buenos Aires. Ed. Palestrina, pp.46-47 (Trans. by L.Chesney).

Steward, J. (ed.) (1949). "The Native Populatio of South America", in: Handbook of South American Indians.Vol.V. Washington.

The United States Bishops'Testimony to Congress (1983). "The United States and Central America". Church in the World. 16.

Vasconi, Tomás (1969). "Dependencia y Superestructura". Rev. Economía y Ciencias Sociales XI. No.3. Caracas. Univ. Central de Venezuela.